DICTIONARY *of*
CANADIANISMS
How to Speak Canadian, *Eh*.

Geordie Telfer

FOLK
LORE
PUBLISHING

The Publisher: Folklore Publishing
Website: www.folklorepublishing.com

Library and Archives Canada Cataloguing in Publication

Telfer, Geordie, 1969–
    Dictionary of Canadianisms: how to speak Canadian, eh! / by Geordie Telfer.

Includes bibliographical references.
ISBN 13: 978-1-894864-85-5

    1. Canadianisms (English)—Dictionaries 2. Canadianisms (English)—Humor. I. Title.

PE3231.T43 2009   422'.97103   C2009-900203-5

Project Director: Faye Boer
Project Editor: Judy Millar
Proofreader: Tracey Comeau
Cover Images: Courtesy of Photos.com

We acknowledge the financial support of the Alberta Foundation for the Arts and the Government of Canada through the Book Publishing Industry Development Program for our publishing activities.

  Canadian Patrimoine
Heritage canadien

PC: P1

Table of Contents

~∞X∞~

Dedicated to
Kim
&
Valin

How to Use This Book

THE FIRST PART of this book is divided into 11 introductory chapters that address a few of the basics of speaking like a Canadian. They cover such topics as how to pronounce ordinary words like a Canadian, how best to describe the weather, how to make yourself understood when ordering in restaurants north of the border and the proper use of "*eh.*" Of particular interest may be the chapter on differences between Canadian English and American English—it may be of use in distinguishing Canadians from Americans (a moot point for most of the rest of the world, but one of fierce pride here at home). By no means are these 11 chapters comprehensive, but whether you're a visitor to the *Great White North* or a lifelong *Canuck*, we hope they'll bring a smile to your lips and a chuckle to your throat.

Part Two, "A Canadian Lexicon," is the actual dictionary of Canadianisms, which, as the book's title has so succinctly promised, is a dictionary of...(wait for it)...Canadianisms. You will have encountered some of these words and phrases in Chapters 1 to 11, but many will be new, some will be old and more than a few will surprise. Use it as you would any dictionary, since it is conveniently arranged in alphabetical order (it may come as a surprise to some, but—yes—we do have alphabetical order in Canada). If you are a visitor to *our home and native land*, the dictionary will help you to better understand the verbal shorthand that Canadians often use to communicate with each other. If you yourself are a Canadian and have purchased this book to read on a plane or simply to give some friend or relative, rest assured that plenty of merriment for word-loving *Canucks* awaits.

Note that words in *italics* (except this one) throughout the book are cross-referenced to words defined in the lexicon.

Happy reading, *eh*?

Introduction

WHAT DOES IT mean to say you are a Canadian?

Writer and historian Pierre Berton famously wrote that a Canadian is somebody who knows how to make love in a canoe. If only it were that easy (and gratifying). Pinning down what makes something "Canadian" or "not Canadian" is a tricky task. Putting together a book that purports to teach people how to speak Canadian (even if only for entertainment purposes) poses some serious questions. How many of the fan favourites do you include just because people expect them—expressions like *double-double, hoser* and *eh*? How far should you go in pointing out the differences between Canadian English and American English—*pop* vs. soda, *running shoes* vs. sneakers, and the proper pronunciation of "lieutenant"? Is it worth mentioning that wherever you go across Canada, a *jelly doughnut* seems to be called something different? How much French should be included given that the book is written in English (if you're new to Canada, this will make no sense)? Is it better to include everyday words that people recognize—like *please, thank you* and *kubasa*—or to emphasize the unusual expressions that readers are less likely to have heard of—*kabluna, cheechako* and *porch-climber*. Do newcomers to Canada today really need to know who *Casey and*

Finnegan were? I have decided that, yes, they do. In fact, this entire book is one Canadian's attempt to wrestle with all the challenges listed above, and more.

Some of the words you will find in the following pages went out of use long ago, but others you may have heard yesterday. Think of this book not so much as a snapshot in time, but rather a beer coaster with some sort of bilingual slogan on it, only about half of which will make any sort of sense (hopefully, the English half). I hope you will enjoy this mixture of old and new, familiar and formal, Canadian and *Canuck*.

–Geordie Telfer

PART ONE

Chapter One

~❊~

Only in Canada, You Say? Pity.

Q: *How many Canadians does it take to screw in a light bulb?*

A: *Four—one to screw in the light bulb and three to point and say, "He's a Canadian."*

IN 2004, *The Canadian Oxford Dictionary* officially added the expression *double-double* to its scholarly pages. An expression long taken for granted by Canadian coffee drinkers as verbal shorthand for "two creams and two sugars," it is hard to believe that *double-double* would even need to be in a dictionary; after all, doesn't everyone know what it means? Don't all English-speaking countries say *double-double*?

Apparently not.

After its inclusion in the dictionary, *double-double* briefly became the "it" word (or words) of the Canadian news cycle. *Double-double* appeared in newspaper stories, was mentioned in radio broadcasts and, for a brief time, was on the lips of anyone interested in words. Once again, Canadians had found something that set them apart from the rest of the world, a small thing to be sure, but nonetheless a puzzler to foreign ears. And then, after being wined and dined by all the linguists, lexicographers and reporters, *double-double* went back to its day job in the coffee shop, serving millions of Canadians who forgot they were even saying it.

Every few years some Canadianism or other gets paraded around like this and then is mercifully let go. In the 1980s it was *eh*, virally spread by the *McKenzie Brothers* with legions of willing carriers; in the 1990s, *Tim Hortons* parlayed its Canadian caché into proud loyalty and even prouder profits; and so, early in the new millennium, it was *double-double*'s turn.

Ask most Canadians and they'll be able to think of at least one or two expressions that are their nominees for the exclusive (yet also polite, modest and funny) "Only in Canada Club." Perhaps for the *Canuck*ophiles among you, all of the following are well-known members of the club: the *Bloody Caesar, ketchup-flavoured chips* and sometimes excessive use of the word *sorry*. But at least some of you probably don't think twice about installing your new *Arborite* counter with *Robertson screws* and then wiping it off with a *J-Cloth* and *Javex*, although you may detect a flutter of delight in the country's collective unconscious as you sip your *Red Rose* tea. Still others go *five-pin bowling* in blissful ignorance, prefer their *Coffee Crisp* and buy their *Smarties* and *Shreddies* at *bargoon* prices. Let's not even get started about St. John vs. St. John's.

Instead, let's begin with *CanCon*, as in:

"The book you are now reading is *CanCon*."

CanCon is short for "Canadian Content" and, difficult as it may be to believe, only Canada has it! *CanCon* means that if you work in media or the arts, the government wants you to create and distribute content (stuff) that reflects Canadian culture. And if you don't know how to do that yourself, you should at least hire another Canadian to do it for you. Usually you have to do it in Canada, but if you're really rich and famous, they'll change the rules to accommodate you. Anyway, *CanCon* is responsible for more than a few of the expressions you will find in this book and is, itself, uniquely Canadian. It makes the perfect jumping-off point for this, Gentle Reader, the beginning of your trek through the wordy wonders of *wild and woolly Canuck*istan.

Chapter Two

~●X●~

Cross Talk
- or -
The Top 10 Differences Between Can-speak and U.S.-speak

FOR MANY CANADIANS, it's not until they talk to an American that they realize how different our vocabularies are. After all, the U.S. is our closest neighbour, our largest trading partner and an undeniable cultural influence; we're inundated with American cars, television, music, fashion and so forth. You'd think that this would mean we'd use all the same words to describe all the same things, but this is not the case.

For instance, upon welcoming an American guest into your typically Canadian home, you may cause some degree of bafflement by saying the following: "Kick off your *running shoes* and have a seat on the *chesterfield*. Sorry about the puddle in front of the door on the way in—I haven't cleaned out the *eavestroughs* yet. Sorry the lights don't work; I haven't paid the *hydro bill*. If you need to go to the washroom, it's right over here. Man, I really have to get this leaky *tap* fixed. Pardon me? You're hungry? Well, I've got a *tin* of soup here somewhere; there's some *pop* in the fridge and some *chocolate bars* on the table."

Okay, so you're not offering your guest the healthiest lunch, nor are you providing a place to stay that has electricity, or even fully functional plumbing. "But," you will ask, "beyond that, what's the problem? All those words in italics are perfectly ordinary." And indeed they are perfectly ordinary—to Canadians. Although we have all the same amenities as Americans (often much to their surprise), in some cases, we use very different words to describe them. Let's pick apart the paragraph above to form an admittedly arbitrary "Top 10 List" of differences between conversational English north and *south of the border*.

#1) *running shoes* vs. "sneakers"

It's not that Canadians or Americans use one or the other exclusively, it's just that Canadians are more likely to say *running shoes*, and Americans are more likely to say "sneakers." In this case at least we'll understand each other; the English-man who approaches, asking where he can buy a pair of "trainers," will likely be greeted with looks of puzzlement from both parties.

#2) *chesterfield* vs. "couch" or "sofa"

Truth be told, this one is starting to fade from general use, even for Canucks. In the 1970s and '80s though, a sure-fire way to pick out a Canadian was the use of *chesterfield*. As you'll see from its entry in the dictionary portion of this book, *chesterfield* is in use in other places around the world, but it is used to refer to a specific kind of multi-person sitting appurtenance, rather than the general use to which Canadians once put it.

#3) *eavestroughs* vs. "rain gutters"

Seeing as how they're troughs that run along the eaves of your house, you'd think the meaning of this would be perfectly obvious, but to Americans, *eavestroughs* sounds like some kind of medieval architecture, and of course knowing about medieval architecture makes us long-haired intellectuals who are therefore dangerous.

#4) *hydro* vs. "electricity"

Usually Canadians have to sit down and seriously explain this one; here, we call electricity *hydro* because, in much of Canada, it's generated by hydroelectric (that is, "water driven") generating stations. But once they know what it means, the term *hydro* seems to make many Americans even more nervous since it suggests the energy they gobble up in such vast quantities actually comes from somewhere and is not a naturally occurring medium such as air or wind.

#5) *go to the washroom* vs. "use the toilet"

Truthfully, many Americans use this phrase as well, but where Canadians are unique is in saying *"go to the washroom"* as a synonym for the act itself instead of the process of travelling to the room in which it is done. So for instance, even on a camping trip, in the middle of nowhere, polite Canadians will still say, "I need to *go to the washroom.*"

#6) *tap* vs. "faucet"

No one knows why, but Canadians are far more likely to say *tap* than "faucet," although of course, many will use both interchangeably. The same goes for Americans, who, though more likely to get the "faucet" fixed, know perfectly well what a glass of tap water is.

#7) *Pardon me?* vs. "What?"

Of course Canadians are not the only ones to say *"Pardon me,"* but north of the border is quickly becoming one of the last places in North America that you may hear this well-mannered query.

And sadly, even in Canada, *pardon me* is slowly falling by the wayside, replaced by the curt and monosyllabic "What?" which has all the grace of a cement block.

#8) *tin* vs. "can"

Canadians will occasionally say *tin* (especially when referring to soup or tuna), but Americans almost never say *tin*, preferring instead, the all-purpose "can."

#9) *pop* vs. "soda"

and ...

#10) *chocolate bar* vs. "candy bar"

Two of the most well-known differences between Canadian and American English, *pop* and *chocolate bar* serve to remind us that many of our linguistic departures describe mundane items of junk food such as *ketchup-flavoured chips*, dill pickle chips, *Jos. Louis* and so forth. However, it is important to note that, in the UK and other Commonwealth countries, Canadians will be perfectly understood if they walk into a grocery store and ask for *Smarties* or *Shreddies*.

Now that we've seen some of the differences in the actual words we speak, the next chapter looks at the way we pronounce our words. Canadians and Americans sometimes butt heads because we simply can't understand one another's vowel sounds, and pretty soon somebody decides they're going to say something about diphthongs and after that, all civility is generally lost.

Onward.

Chapter Three

~⚬✕⚬~

Vowel Movements and Other Discomforts
- or -
What Is a Diphthong Anyway?

THERE'S "NO DOUBT ABOUT IT," Canadians have a distinctive way of speaking. In fact, depending on
what part of Canada you're from, some critics
will insist that you're actually saying, "Noo doot
aboot it" or perhaps, "No doat aboat it." Indeed,
Canada is so vast and its people so diverse that
our speech offers considerable differences to our
own ears, let alone those of visiting outsiders.
Instead of focusing on the words themselves, this
chapter looks at how we say them and how our
pronunciation differs not only from those nether

regions we call *south of the border* but also within *our home and native land*.

Without getting into linguistic mumbo-jumbo like "alveolar consonants" and "flapping intervocalics," there are a couple of terms you'll need to be familiar with. The first is "diphthong." Despite its suggestive spelling, a diphthong has nothing to do with the stringy underwear so popular among those who enjoy adventures in *gitch*, nor does it have anything to do with the respiratory illness diphtheria. (This writer suggests that, if you are so unlucky as to have diphtheria, slipping into a thong is probably the last thing on your mind.) In fact, a diphthong is the sound two vowels make together; for instance, the word "sound" itself contains an "ou" diphthong that is very easy to hear, whereas the word "hear" contains a much subtler "ea" diphthong.

The second term you'll need to know is "Canadian raising." Canadian raising does not refer to one's upbringing in the *Great White North*, nor does it refer to *raised chocolate* or *maple* icing on *doughnuts*. Canadian raising is the name that linguists have given to the way that we pronounce vowels and therefore—you guessed it—diphthongs. Armed with this crucial knowledge, we can now proceed to the matter at hand.

When they aren't busy making fun of us for having universal *health care* and the *metric system*, Americans prone to poking fun tend to pick on

the ways that Canadians pronounce their diphthongs. For some reason, the famous example is
the phrase "out and about in a boat." *Yankees*
think that *Canucks* are saying "oot and aboot in
a boot" (all rhyming with "loot") or sometimes
"oat and aboat in aboat" (all rhyming with "boat").
Meanwhile, to Canadian ears, it may sound like
the *Yankee* interloper is saying "owt and abowt in
a boat" (the first two words rhyming with "owl,"
"wow," "how," etc., and the "boat" being pronounced more or less recognizably). Similarly,
mid-westerners will pronounce "house" not to
rhyme with "mouse" (as it does for Canadians), but
with the diphthong sound found in the words
"sound" and "found"; to delicate Canadian ears it
sounds like "how-oose." And if the house has a roof,
the "oo" will not sound like "truth," but rather "push,"
with the speaker's "ruf" suggesting a rather unimag-
inative impression of a mid-sized dog.

Once you've exhausted all the weird things
Americans do to diphthongs, you're left with
their shameless mangling of hapless individual
vowels. For instance, Canadians are often shocked
and dismayed to learn that many Americans pronounce "writer" to rhyme with "rider," whereas
Canadians will pronounce "writer" to rhyme with
"lighter," and "rider" to rhyme with "wider." And
for central Canadians who live near the border,
watching a TV broadcast from Buffalo can be
a painful experience, as the short "o" sound of

"not" is ruthlessly amputated to the short "a" sound of "nat": "Bob got hot in his hat" is pronounced "Babb gat hat in his hee-at." To many Canadian ears, this bizarre and uncalled for assault on the English language sounds cheap and tacky.

Aside from vowels that are routinely pronounced differently, individual words also seem to obey a different set of laws depending on which side of the border they're spoken. For instance, the innocent and cost-saving "coupon" is pronounced "koo-pawn" in Canada but in some regions of the U.S. emerges as the genteelly, dainty sounding "kew-pawn." Americans, who quite sensibly pronounce "lieutenant" as "loo-tenant" are understandably baffled by the phantom "f" that Canadians add to say "leff-tenant." Canadians, with the influence of the French, know that the "er" in "foyer" means it should be pronounced "foy-ay," while Americans likely miss more than a few cross-border appointments because they are waiting in the "foy-ur." When Americans ask what progress has been made, they enigmatically refer to something called "praw-gress," oddly familiar to Canadians who may be more accustomed to "proh-gress." And finally, although Canadians may be more prone to say "eye-ther" and Americans "eee-ther," in truth, both say either.

But enough about the U.S. What about regional differences heard here at home? There's no shame in admitting that some of the diphthong exaggerations noted by Americans actually do have a basis in truth. The "oat and aboat in a boat" pronunciation seems to pop up more often in northern and rural communities, while "oot and aboot in a boot" is generally less frequent, but far more noticeable. The reasons for this could lie in Canada's Scottish heritage and the Scots English drawl of "Now, laddie…" into "Newww, laddie…" Old habits die hard…

And of course there are other differences, each generally only discernible to Canadians not from the area in question. East Coasters can often be picked out by the breathy consonant "t" at the end of words like "hot" and "shut" as well as sometimes pronouncing the "u" sound in "but" like "book." In Québec, of course, many different pronunciations are at work, both in the speaking of French and consequently of English. Perhaps the most often stereotyped quirk of English-speaking French Canadians is the tendency to add an "h" sound to the front of words beginning with vowels, thus transmuting "I fell on my ass at centre ice" into "High fell hon my hass hat centre hice." And a word of warning to pidgin-French speakers visiting Québec; if you have only rudimentary high-school French, you may best make yourself understood by simply speaking English while adopting an exaggerated French Canadian accent.

As one creeps towards the centre of the country, there is a tendency to drop the "h" sound as well as skipping mid-word vowels and consonants. This means that the query: "Where are you headed?" and the accompanying response, "Toronto," would actually be rendered: "Where y'edded?" with the answer, "T'ranna." And of course, from Labrador to BC, the crisp, carefully enunciated consonants and full-throated vowels of *First Nations* peoples lends a rich undertone to a nation often too busy being "oat and aboat" to notice its own linguistic heritage.

As with so many of the things that make Canada distinct, we don't usually appreciate our idiosyncrasies until we travel away from them. It's not until we hear unfamiliar tongues tripping over commonplace words like *poutine* ("pootin"), *Nanaimo bars* ("Ninnymoe bars") and *Nunavut* ("none of it") that we realize we have indeed travelled far from home. And sometimes it is this longing for familiar voices and friendly accents that leads us back again.

Chapter Four

～❊～

How's It Goin', Eh?

eh *interjection informal* 1. inviting assent *("nice day, eh?")* 2. *Cdn.* ascertaining the comprehension, continued interest, agreement, etc. of the person or persons addressed *("It's way out in the suburbs, eh, so I can't get there by bike.")*

–*The Canadian Oxford Dictionary*, 2nd Ed.

BY FAR THE MOST well-known Canadianism is *eh*. Rightly or wrongly, Canadians have been stereotyped as inserting this tiny word into the most unlikely (and sometimes unwelcome) places. For example, "I'm writing a book, *eh*, and it's about Canadian English, *eh*?" The exact reason for the viral spread of *eh* will never be known, but we can at least track its use through time and try to determine where it came from. We can also engage in a bit of myth-busting to see if *eh* is used as often today as it once, if ever, was.

In 1981, *Bob & Doug McKenzie* released their album, *Great White North*. To the delight of *doughnut*-shop denizens, beer-store buddies and legions of *lumberjacket*-wearing teens, Canada's *hosers* had found their voice, and the voice said *eh*. In truth, the *McKenzies'* creators, Rick Moranis and Dave Thomas, were simply capitalizing on what had previously been a minor, if widely recognized, oddity of Canadian English. However, combined with the fact that plenty of Canadians were saying it already, the runaway success of the *Great White North* album meant that even more people started peppering their speech with errant *ehs*. Young people especially, many of whom previously had no idea that *eh* was what Canadians were supposed to say, happily embraced it as an informal handshake that immediately made everyone feel at home, either in a group of new people or among old friends. More than ever it had become a way to say, "I'm Canadian like you, *eh*?" with no need for the actual words "I'm Canadian like you."

~✣~

When did all this *eh* business begin anyway? Writers and linguists started writing about *eh* as a distinctly Canadian trait in the 1950s. In 1959, the *Journal of the Canadian Linguistic Association* published an article by Harold B. Allen entitled "Canadian-American Speech Differences Along the Middle Border." Allen asserts that *eh* is "so exclusively a Canadian feature that immigration officials use it as an identifying clue." And Professor Walter S. Avis, who later edited the scholarly *A Dictionary of Canadianisms on Historical Principles* (a *Centennial* project if ever there was one), writes that he had started to comment on *eh* in lectures and broadcasts around the mid-1950s.

By 1971, *eh* was so widely identified with Canadian English that Professor Avis contributed an article to *The Canadian Journal of Linguistics* entitled, "So eh is Canadian, eh?" In the article, he demonstrates that the word *eh* is not an exclusively Canadian phenomenon (which of course it isn't) and then goes on to show that particular *uses* of *eh* actually *are* distinctly Canadian. What does all this mean? Well, here goes.

Avis cites a variety of literary sources to entertainingly prove that *eh* has seen plenty of action both in the UK and the U.S. (mainly in the north).

For instance, when the character Hippolito cannot believe what he has just heard in Thomas Dekker's 1604 play *The Honest Whore*, he exclaims, "Ay? It cannot be..." Or when Sir Leicester in Charles Dickens' 1852 novel *Bleak House* fails to hear the person addressing him, he cries, "Eh?" Now, both of these uses of *eh* (or "ay") represent honest queries for further information. In the majority of his examples, Avis shows that *eh* is usually used to invite some sort of response, even if that response is not expected to be given, for example: "...maybe you'll be going to the West Indies again some day, eh?" (*Westward Ho!* by UK writer Charles Kingsley, 1855); "Busy as usual, eh?" (*Ten Nights in a Bar-Room*, by U.S. writer William W. Pratt, 1858); or "Listen, Harry, phone me before you go out tonight, eh?" (*Strange Fugitive*, by Canadian writer Morley Callaghan, 1928).

There are, however, two uses of *eh* for which Avis can only cite Canadian (or mostly Canadian) examples, and these are:

Reinforcing an imperative command: You can look to the example by Callaghan, above, or consider "'Yeh, I know,' Aunt Edna sounded annoyed. 'But let me say it, eh?'" (*A Bird in the House*, by Canadian writer Margaret Laurence, 1963–67).

The narrative *eh*?: To illustrate a use of *eh* probably familiar to Canadians today, Avis offers the following example: "He's holding on to a fire hose, *eh*? The thing is jumping all over the place, *eh*, and he can hardly hold on to it, *eh*? Well he finally loses control of it, *eh*, and the water knocks down half a dozen bystanders."

Soaked bystanders notwithstanding, it is rare at the time of writing (2009) to hear the narrative *eh* used so frequently, but more on this later.

From his 1971 vantage point, Avis also writes that while "the narrative *eh* is probably not a recent innovation, it has certainly increased in intensity in the last decade. In many situations it parallels that of 'see?' and 'you know?', both of which intrude habitually in the narrative style of some speakers, especially the little educated." And so we start to see a scenario in which Canadians began using *eh* as a way of inviting agreement, but over a decade or two, turned it in to a flavouring word to which no response is required.

The story doesn't end here, however. In the same way that the use of *eh* evolved between 1959 and 1971, it has continued to grow and expand to the present day. In 2004, Elaine Gold conducted a survey of students at the University of Toronto to assess current use of *eh*. To formulate her questions, Gold delineated a new list of *eh* usage that reflected its modern use. It is interesting to note how much our awareness and use of *eh* seems to have increased since 1971.

Type of *eh*	Sample Sentence
1. Statements of opinion	Nice day, eh?
2. Statements of fact	It goes over here, eh?
3. Commands	Open the window, eh? Think about it, eh?
4. Exclamations	What a game, eh?
5. Questions	What are they trying to do, eh?
6. To mean *pardon*.	Eh? What did you say?
7. In fixed expressions	Thanks, eh? I know, eh?
8. Insults	You're a real snob, eh?
9. Accusations	You took the last piece, eh?
10. Storytelling (the narrative *eh* referred to by Avis)	This guy is up on the 27th floor, eh? then he gets out on the ledge, eh...

Gold found that the top three usages that her respondents had reported hearing were, "Nice day, eh?" "What a game, eh?" and "I know, eh?" And when responding to which *ehs* they themselves most often used, the results were very similar, with the top three being, "I know, eh?" "Nice day, eh?" and "What a game, eh?" Interestingly, 92 percent of female respondents reported using "I know, eh?" themselves, compared to 72 percent for males. The reason this is worth noting is that *eh* is so often seen to be the word of choice for **male**, flannel-shirt clad *hosers*. Compared to a similar survey done in Vancouver and Ottawa in 1980, Gold found that *eh* seems to be used far more often in central Canada than in the west. And *The Canadian Oxford Dictionary* cites Manitoba and New Brunswick as mighty bastions of *eh* use. Furthermore, Gold found that when comparing the 1980 results from Ottawa and the 2004 results from Toronto, the use and acceptance of *eh* (in cases like "Nice day, eh?") had stayed about the same, but use of the narrative *eh* actually appeared to have increased.

It remains unclear what we are to make of this. In yet another set of interviews at U of T, sociolinguist Sali Tagliamonte posits that the use of *eh* is actually in decline, especially in Canadian cities. Young people no longer bandy it about because it sounds uneducated and is associated with rural areas (for kids, the very antithesis of a presumed hip-urban lifestyle). Tagliamonte further suggests that most uses of *eh* in an urban environment are by older people who have moved to the city from a rural environment.

From this writer's perspective (a university-educated male, born in 1969 and having lived in Toronto his entire life) use of the narrative *eh*

("He's holding on to a fire hose, *eh*? The thing is jumping all over the place, *eh*" etc.) has certainly decreased since going to a suburban high school in the mid-1980s. However, uses such as "I know, eh?" are still heard so often that one barely even notices any more.

What seems unchanged about *eh* is that Canadians react very differently to its use. Some happily embrace it as a unique badge of national identity. Others simply accept it as a fact of life. And yet others still regard *eh* as "a pernicious carbuncle" on the fresh face of Canadian English.

Chapter Five

~❦~

Spell Like a Canadian
- or -
O-U Don't Say!

THIS IS GOING to be a short chapter; however, it has hum**our**, col**our** and will keep its hon**our** intact even as it pl**oughs** forward, occasionally veering to the left of cent**re**. Astute readers will have already seen where this is leading; that is, a brief survey of the murky vortex in which Canadian, British and American spelling all come together. Herein you will find age-old rivalries: "ou" vs. "o"; titanic clashes: "ough" vs. "ow"; and cataclysmic battles: "re" vs. "er." Let's get to it, shall we?

The difference familiar to most Canadians is our retention of the British "ou" instead of just "o" in words such as labour, neighbour, favour and countless others. It may come as a shock to learn that, until 1990, Canadian newspapers habitually used the American spellings, but in that fateful year, the *Globe and Mail* courageously acquiesced to years of reader complaints and switched to Canadian spellings. Other newspaper and news services followed suit as the decade unfolded.

There is no great mystery as to the "why" of the "ou" phenomenon—the British did it, they still do it and so do we. But it merits mention here because it is a Canadianism many people encounter in daily life, especially those who use word processing programs with self-correcting spelling features. There's nothing more annoying than typing a simple, businesslike sentence— "My new cheques have arrived, but they are grey in colour instead of black, and my name is off-centre."—only to see it emerge as a red-streaked variation of the following: "My new cheques have arrived but they are grey in colour instead of black, and my name is off-centre." Depending on what software you're using (Canada doesn't constitute a large enough market to have its own word processing software), the program may even save you the trouble of correcting your atrocious spelling and make the correction for you, because surely that was what you wanted it to do. This sort of thing is particularly frustrating if you're writing a book about how to speak (or spell) Canadian.

Another of our borrowings from the British (though some would argue it seems suspiciously French) is the use of "re" instead of "er." The most common instance of this is in the word "centre," but another notable instance occurs in the spelling of the common metric units of measurement: millimetres, centimetres, metres and kilometres. Aside from Liberia and Myanmar, the U.S. is the only country in the world not to have adopted the metric system, but this doesn't stop its uppity word processing programs from insisting that millimetres, centimetres, metres and kilometres are the spellings the rest of the world ought to adopt. It is in vain that one points out its name is the metric system and not the meteric system, or from a Canadian point of view, the meteric system.

As well as the systemic spelling differences between Canada and the U.S., a few other odd-ball spellings must be taken into consideration; among these are "grey" vs. "gray," "cheque" vs. "check" and "through" vs. the occasional use of the informal "thru." It was certainly not my intent to turn these introductory chapters into a rant on American spelling and pronunciation, but I cannot deny that this seems to be what has happened. From a linguistic point of view, our differences must be measured largely against the U.S., since our two countries are the only two English-speaking nations in the Americas. And in that respect, as we do over so many other matters, we shall have to continue to agree to disagree, looking for new ways to work through our differences and not thru them.

Chapter Six

~⚛~

Hosers, Chowderheads and Mangia Cakes - or - How We Insult Ourselves and Others

CANADIANS HAVE A REPUTATION the world over for being polite. In part, this is because of our frequent and willing use of the phrases "thank you," "excuse me," "you're welcome," and of course, the ubiquitous *sorry*. But while we may be relatively polite in our day-to-day dealings both here at home and in foreign lands, when the occasion arises, Canadians can be insulting and rude right up there with the best of them. A word of warning though: the insults that follow are not necessarily for everyday use. Some of them are obscure regional sayings while others apply only to very specific situations. And if you are a visitor to Canada, planning to pull one of these out of your holster, be forewarned—eyebrows may be raised, not because the particular insult you have chosen is exceptionally rude, but simply because the intended recipient may not have heard it before.

General insults from our multicultural society

hoser: A general insult, but especially appropriate when addressing an uncouth (and probably beer-swilling, baseball cap-wearing, hockey-watching) lout whom you wish to call a goof, loser, and so on. It is particularly useful because *hosers* themselves know what it means and often use it with each other: "You hoser!" "You're a hoser." "No, you're a hoser." "No, you're a—" Well, you get the idea.

lederhoser: This term, of relatively recent coinage, describes a Canadian of arguably dubious mental competency who insists on wearing shorts out of doors during our coldest winter months.

chowderhead: A priceless treasure from the Maritimes, appropriate for use all across the country. Without putting too fine a point on it, calling someone a *chowderhead* is simply a soupy way of calling them dumb.

mangia cake: In the multicultural utopia that is Canada, at some point the Italians came up with this one to denigrate the sissified customs of non-Italians, especially those of British decent. It means "cake eater." However, as so often happens, the *mangia cakes* themselves (the non-Italians, especially of British descent) took it, mispronounced it "mawnjee cake" and started using it themselves to describe anyone thought to be a sissy, bourgeois milquetoast, uptight *anglo*, etc. (though we have the French to thank for *anglo*). "Come on y'buncha *mangia cakes*; take off your clothes and jump into the freezing lake."

kabluna: This Inuktitut zinger means *Big Eyebrow* and stems from early Inuit encounters with Europeans, who presumably had big eyebrows. While it is not overtly hostile, it has the potential for a pleasingly downputting tone. "I just sold the *kabluna* a refrigerator!"

cheechako: A *Chinook* jargon term for "newcomer" that can be used as either a noun or an adjective. Like *kabluna*, it can also be a simple description without necessarily being offensive; for instance, "*Chimo*, my *cheechako* friend." vs. "These *cheechakos* are *slocums*."

A few gems from "la belle province"

It should come as no surprise that French Canadians have their own special ways of insulting one another. When translated into English, many of these phrases become funnier than they likely are in French. It is also debatable how often Québecers and other francophones actually use these expressions in everyday conversation, but nonetheless they are jibes worthy of note.

To begin with, let us say that you find yourself in a situation that calls for you to tell someone to "bug-off," "stop bothering me" or "kiss my ass." Any of the following Gallic jibes may suffice:

French	English translation
Va pèter dans le trèfle	Go fart in the clover
Mange-toi du pain blanc	Eat white bread
Baise-moué l'ail	Kiss my garlic

Or let us suppose that you are looking for a colourful, folksy way of saying, "shut-up." You can immediately trot out this rustic-sounding chestnut:

Ferme ton gorlot. "Shut your sleigh bell."

Québecers who wish to impugn someone else's worthiness as French Canadians have any number of trenchant witticisms at their disposal, but two of the best are:

French	English translation
vendu	Literally meaning "sold," this noun describes a French Canadian thought to have "sold out" to the ways of the *anglos* and is a grave affront.
joual	Stemming from the pronunciation of "cheval" (horse), this describes

uneducated, poorly spoken Québecers who "speak like horses."

Insults and jibes for specific occasions

While run-of-the-mill curses and insults are fine, sometimes you just need more. The table below provides a handy reference guide for either situation and how you can best offend those involved, all the while adopting an appropriate vocabulary of mockery.

Occasion/ Circumstance/ Person	Insult
cranky individual quick to anger	*a temper in search of a tantrum*
obsequious ass-kisser	*browner*
gossip	*clap-dish*
a person who needlessly fusses	*clucker*
an absent skill or talent	*future strength*
clothing that is in poor taste	*I wouldn't wear that to a dogfight*
serial bedder of hockey players	*puck bunny*
self-righteous teetotaller	*pump sucker*
someone now enjoying a more licentious life than before	*pure as the driven snow but drifted*

someone who is very talkative	*talks the nuts off a steel bridge*
the absence of manners	*Were you born in a sawmill!?*
Canadian who adopts American ways	*whitewashed American*
inquiry as to why someone is in a bad mood	*Who peed in your cornflakes this morning?*
unwanted persistence	*you can't keep a good dog off your leg*

The Presumed Lack of Mental Acuity

There are many different but equally unflattering expressions to describe people seen as being, to put it bluntly, dumb.

The expressions listed below are by no means a complete list of all the similar terms found in this book (after all, the dictionary portion should leave some things to be discovered). But they all seem to share a certain joy in colourfully characterizing Canadians who are slow on the uptake. After all, it's a harsh environment we live in (except for Vancouver), and doing something stupid (like not dressing for the weather) can result in death.

It is hardly surprising then that some of these phrases bear the hallmarks of having been carefully crafted during long winter months in anticipation of the next time you see your slow-witted neighbour (which might not be until the spring thaw).

dumb as two short planks
empty barrels make the most noise
good head for bouncing bricks off
no grain in that silo
not much upstairs
sharp as a beach ball

And finally, two useful epithets for hurling an un-fond farewell

Don't change. I wanna forget you just as you are.
Come back again when you can't stay so long.

Chapter Seven

∽♋∾

The Northern Gourmet
- or -
"You got your bannock in my cretons!"
"You got your cretons on my bannock!"
"Wow! Two great tastes that taste great together!"

WHILE FEW WOULD DENY that Canada has a national cuisine, most would be hard-pressed to specify what exactly it is. Many will immediately think of the daunting meal known as the *lumberjack's breakfast*, complete with eggs, ham, bacon (Canadian or otherwise), hash browns, pancakes or waffles and generally accompanied by a generous flask of *maple syrup* (whose flavour, it should be noted, also complements bacon and ham). If you're in Québec, you can look for a little *cretons* on the side, but once you've had breakfast, how is one to eat like a Canadian for the rest of the day?

The uninitiated gastronome in the *Great White North* will run into difficulties. For instance, let us suppose that after breakfast you decide to have a coffee and a *doughnut* to keep you going until lunchtime. When ordering at your local *doughnut* shop, your polite request for a *double-double* will almost certainly be universally understood, but if you decide to order something simple like a *jelly doughnut*, you will have entered deep waters. For instance, if you are in Alberta or Saskatchewan, your simple *jelly doughnut* is properly called a *bismarck*. However, if you are in Manitoba, you must order a *jambuster*, since your request for a *bismarck* will get you not a *jelly doughnut*, but instead, the chocolate-glazed, cream-filled confection known in Ontario as a *Bavarian cream* (note that both the terms *bismarck* and *Bavarian cream* would seem to suggest some common Teutonic influence). Of course, you could override all these difficulties by simply requesting a *jelly doughnut* since this term is generally understood, if not always used.

If something as simple as ordering a *doughnut* can be this complicated for Canadians themselves, imagine what ordering in restaurants must be like for visitors from foreign lands, in particular, the foreign land of America. For instance, our American cousins may not realize that in Canada, it is more appropriate to order "supper" instead of "dinner," although either one will be perfectly understood. Supposing that our American cousins have decided to order a hamburger with bacon and cheese, their request for a "bacon cheese-burger" will be easily comprehended, but they will not realize that *banquet burger* is what we call it up here in Canada. Furthermore, they may request "American cheese," which, to Canadians, is a rubberized edible petroleum product called *process(ed) cheese*. Visitors from *south of the border* may also be puzzled when their server offers to get them fresh *cutlery* (instead of "silverware") wrapped in a *serviette* (instead of a "napkin"). The final faux pas of course is asking for the "check" and not the *bill*, although this may first be preceded by the penultimate faux pas of pronouncing "faux pas" as "fokes pass."

❧❦❧

The true national cuisine of Canada is, like Canada itself, a hodgepodge of dishes, treats and snacks influenced by cooking from all over the world, but finally created and enjoyed right here at home. In fact, so diverse are Canada's meals and the names we call them, it is probably safe to say that if you've heard of half of them, you're doing well. The regional favourites that follow combine tastes both familiar and new, *as well* as sensations both sweet and savoury.

So tuck in your *serviette* and pull out your *cutlery* as we chart a...

First course north of the 49th parallel

baker's fog/boughten: Canadians like their bread, and these two terms hail from the East Coast and the Prairies respectively, to describe store-bought bread seen to be either less substantial or simply inferior to its home-baked counterpart. The first is a noun, "This *baker's fog* is awful," while the second is an adjective, "This *boughten* bread bites!"

bannock: Heavy bread originating in and associated with the far north, suitable for use on the trail or at home.

brewis: Pronounced "brooze," this Newfoundland soul food consists of bread or a biscuit boiled in fatty broth until it is a thick stew, which is then eaten with breakfast in much the same way beans may be eaten with bangers and mash.

bush salmon: BC slang for poached deer. Any attempt to order this in a restaurant will be rightly met by bemused looks of non-comprehension because, even if your server knows what it is to begin with, the odds of a restaurant serving deer are slim, while the odds of a restaurant serving poached deer are even slimmer yet, and finally, the odds of a restaurant serving poached deer and admitting to it are almost non-existent.

cipaille: Thick, savoury pie made from alternating layers of meat and pastry. It marks one of the rare cases in which an English term "sea-pie" has been bastardized by the French to *cipaille.* It remains unclear as to whether the ingredients ever included seafood. Perhaps it marks French Canada's response to the denigrating *Frenchman's turkey* (see below).

Frenchman's turkey: On PEI, a fish dinner usually consisting of herring and having nothing to do with fowl. A not-so-subtle jab at the French.

holubtsi: One might just as easily call this "Little Cabbage Roll on the Prairie" for that is exactly what it is. Pronounced "HOLL-up-chee," this Ukrainian favourite is prairie comfort food for both Ukrainians and non-Ukrainians alike.

kubasa: A hearty sausage seen as a mainstay of Ukrainian communities in the prairies. While it is known and enjoyed across North America (and Europe, of course), for Canadians, *kubasa* has come to be a beloved emblem of transplanted Ukrainian culture.

un 'ot dog/steamie: If you are visiting Québec and want to order a hot dog, you should under no circumstances ask for "un chien chaud" which, although it be a literally correct translation, is simply not what they are called in Québec. Instead you should ask for "un 'ot dog" or "un steamie."

poutine: Rightly hailed as a sort of Canadian ambrosia, this mixture of French fries, cheese-curds and gravy is a true Canadian invention. It is not recommended for those with high cholesterol.

scruncheons: These bits of animal fat or fish liver with the oil rendered out are so highly valued as food they are also thrown on the fire when fuel is running low.

Dessert in Canuckistan

blueberry grunt: Happily, the name of this Maritime dessert does not refer to the sounds that people make while eating it, but rather the sound the boiling pot makes during the preparation of this blueberry dumpling confection.

Cape Breton pork pie: A dessert made of dates, contained by pastry. Seemingly a dig at either the intellect or the taste buds of Cape Bretoners.

figgy-duff: Although it sounds like the name of some whimsical character in a storybook for British school children ("The Adventures of *Figgy Duff* in the Crumpet Barrow"), this is actually a dessert made of raisins and boiled dough, often associated with Newfoundland.

Jos. Louis cakes: Invented in Québec, and now available in almost any Canadian convenience store, these treats consist of a layer of vanilla cream sandwiched between two thin chocolate cakes, the whole being coated in a thin layer of chocolate. If you're really not concerned about your health, one of these is the perfect chaser to a plate of *poutine*.

Nanaimo bars: While they may or may not have been invented in Nanaimo, BC, these delicious squares can be found in bake sales and kitchens all across the country. They consist of a bottom layer of cookie crumbs and chocolate covered in a vanilla butter-cream filling, all of these layers being capped in a thickish layer of chocolate.

Coffee Crisp: A brand name of chocolate bar until recently only available in Canada and consisting of several layers of thin wafers sandwiching layers of coffee cream and coated in chocolate.

Not-so-fine French cuisine

Even Canadians who don't speak a word of French, when pressed, can probably mispronounce the names of their favourite foods en français. This is because all of our food labels and packaging include English on one side and French on the other. In fact, Canadians who **think** they can speak French, when asked to do so, will often blurt out a few random food phrases, such as the following:

beignes: Doughnuts. When you're running late for work and you're jogging along with your box of sugar-coated peace offerings, you can ponder this word, know it, love it and gobble one up before you even arrive.

beurre d'arachides: Peanut butter, not to be confused with spider butter, which would be "beurre d'arachnides" (not really, but "beurre d'araignées" just doesn't sound the same).

jus d'ananas: Pineapple juice. If there were any justice in the world for dyslexics, this would actually mean "Just bananas," but there isn't, so it doesn't.

meilleur avant: Best before.

pamplemousse: Grapefruit. If you've just driven across the border into Québec and want to shout out something boisterous in French, roll down the window and shout this at attractive members of whichever sex you're attracted to. They'll think you're nuts, but if you bump into them later, at least they'll remember you.

fèves au lard: Beans with pork. No matter which language you say it in, this tinned staple would be more accurately described as "a tin full of beans with a microscopic particle of bacon rind floating around somewhere."

sirop d'érable: French for "maple syrup," this is a phrase that even non-French-speaking Americans may recognize since many of them have purchased souvenir tins of it that sit unopened on kitchen windowsills.

tire sur la neige: A traditional winter treat consisting of heated *maple syrup* poured onto snow, which is then eaten as the syrup cools. The good news is that if you're out hunting and realize that you've forgotten to catch dessert, you can whip something up with little more than a campfire, some syrup and a bit of snow. (Hint: Snow that is not yellow tastes better.)

Canada's cuisine is a reflection of our national character; that is, variously salty, sweet, plain and, occasionally, bitter. Similarly, the words we use to describe our cuisine are salty, sweet, plain and occasionally bitter. While haute cuisine has its place, the dishes we associate most with our great nation are the ones that offer up savoury regional specialties with functional (if evocative) names. Often these dishes are made from simple ingredients, lovingly prepared and joyously consumed. And delicious though they may be, they also serve as hearty fuel for the many rigours of everyday life in our great nation, which for most Canadians, of course, include felling trees, building igloos, seal hunting and paddling a hundred kilometers in a day to get your furs to the depot on time.

Bon appétit!

Chapter Eight

Weather

IN 1753, THE FRENCH PHILOSOPHER, writer and all-round Enlightenment *shit disturber*, François-Marie Arouet (better known as "Voltaire"), wrote that Canada was nothing more than "a country covered with snows and ices eight months out of the year." Now, more than 200 years later, it is fashionable to say that Canada is *nine months of winter and three of poor skating* (depending on how long winter is where you live). No fan of the *true north strong and free*, Voltaire was at it again in his 1758 novel *Candide*, dismissively referring to

Canada as "a few acres of snow" (quelques arpents de neige). Not to be outdone by some *hoser* like Voltaire, in the early 1980s the *McKenzie Brothers* popularized the moniker *Great White North* in majestic (and mocking) reference to *our home and native land's* vast, snow-covered expanses.

The point here is that, whether you're Voltaire or *Bob & Doug McKenzie*, Canada's climate has long been used to characterize the country. Voltaire's dislike of Canada wasn't personal; he just didn't think it was worth France's while to squander its resources in trying to colonize "some savage lands somewhere around *Acadia*." And since then, the general assumption that Canada is a snowy fortress of icy solitude has found favour with many, especially those who do not actually live here. Of course, unless you reside in Vancouver or Victoria, Canada's winters can be, and often are, epic marathons of human endurance in the face of overwhelmingly hostile natural elements. It is not for nothing that the hardiest of the *voyageurs*, who worked through the winter, were respectfully referred to as "l'hivernants." In fact, if you've ever taken one of those English classes where the teacher talks about "man vs. nature," this is it.

But having said all that, it must be remembered that most of Canada's population lives in clumps closer to the 49th parallel than not. This means that, rather than enduring a year-long winter of darkness and snow, many Canadians actually get to experience the different seasons and all the variety they bring. Small wonder, then, that there is no shortage of words and expressions to describe Canada's often contradictory climate.

General descriptions of various kinds of weather

open and shut day: As the weather forecasters say, "Cloudy with sunny periods."

Don't like the weather? Just wait five minutes.: A rhetorical phrase often heard in Vancouver and Calgary because so many of those cities' residents have experienced sun, clouds, rain, snow and hail, all in the same five-minute drive.

not too bad of a day: A most useful phrase since it may refer to an exceptionally fine day with pleasant weather. Or, in an exemplary instance of Canadian understatement, it may refer to an incredibly cold or foul day.

(the) old woman's plucking her geese today: A colourful expression to describe big, fat snow flakes falling like clumps of eiderdown from the leaden skies above.

mauzy: Damp, foggy or misty weather.

not a fit day for a fence post (a day not fit for a fence post): Eschewing the ambiguity of *not too bad of a day*, this phrase leaves no doubt about it—the weather is really bad and you don't want to be out in it. In fact, even your fence posts (presumably used to all sorts of weather) should be lavished with sympathy on a day such as this.

snotty: Wet or drizzly weather, either similar in atmospheric consistency to snot, or inspiring the drippage of same.

The changing of the seasons (and ways to celebrate the lack thereof)

Although Canadians are glad for the occasional change of season, most agree that it often takes a frustratingly long time for such changes to come about. And so, not only do we have special names for these times of year but also a multitude of celebrations to mark either the end of winter or to defiantly celebrate its longevity. So brush up on your ice-carving skills and get ready to party.

Carnaval: Carnaval is Québec City's way of bridging the mid-winter blahs between the end of January and the beginning of February. As the world's largest winter carnival, it is a happy celebration of winter itself at a time when many Canadians are feeling ready for winter to be over.

Winterlude: Not to be outdone by Québec City in showing a hardy love of winter, the cities of Ottawa and Gatineau uphold the honour of Ontario and the rest of Québec with their joint celebration of *Winterlude* during the last three weeks of February. There will be skating; there will be ice-sculpting; you will be cold.

flower count: While the rest of Canada is still digging out from the snow (and pretending to like it), the residents of balmy Victoria rub it in by staging a February photo-op known as the *flower count.* Victorians scurry about counting all the flowers already blooming while the rest of the country ignores them and gets back to shovelling.

Reading Week: A week-long break for Canadian university students, usually during late February or early March. Some students diligently catch up on reading and assignments while most others breathe a sigh of relief and take a break from their strenuous winter term (sometimes flying off to warmer climes or going home for a visit).

March break: A week-long break for students in public and high schools, sometimes celebrated by parents with family trips to warm climates. While the weather in much of Canada is still miserable and slushy (if not downright arctic) during the March break, for many it marks the first intimation that winter may not last forever. It is not to be confused with the U.S. "spring break" during which university students fly south for drunken revelry and intimate, if casual, relations.

Toonik tyme: A springtime festival held in Iqaluit to celebrate the return of the sun after long months of winter darkness. If anyone has reason to celebrate the beginning of the end of winter, the residents of Canada's far north must surely stake the most righteous claim.

How many words for snow?

According to a spurious urban legend, the Inuit have more than 100 different words for "snow." In fact, this is not the case; furthermore, they do not have 50, 30 or even 20. What the various Inuit languages and dialects do have, however, is a very complex system of adding suffixes to the ends of words, so that in much the same way that the English language can have "snow storms," "snow squalls," "snow falls" and "snow days," so too do the languages of the far north have many different ways of modifying the root word for "snow." However, upon journeying into English-speaking Canada, it is amusing to note that there are plenty of different terms for rain and especially ice, a few of which are offered below for your consideration.

Rain

blueberry run: A heavy rain that washes away ripe blueberries. It should be noted that this term can also refer to diarrhea caused by eating too many blueberries.

drash of rain: A sudden, heavy shower of rain.

gullywasher: A very heavy rain.

poor man's fertilizer: A late spring rainfall that waters the crops.

Ice

(heard mostly in Atlantic Canada)

ballicatter: Distinctive-looking ice that forms along the shoreline from the crashing of waves during freezing temperatures.

frazil: When moving water is not still enough to completely freeze, it forms this slushy mixture that is highly unpleasant to walk through or fall into. See also, *lolly*, *slob ice* and *slurry* below.

ice pan: A broad sheet or chunk of floating ice (and sometimes used as the foundation for a nice, safe game of *steppycock*).

lolly: Floating slushy ice, for all intents and purposes identical to *frazil*, *slob ice* and *slurry*.

rotten ice: Ice that was once solid and still looks solid on top, but has in fact thawed into a treacherous morass. It is particularly dangerous on lakes and frozen inlets where unwary folk may fall into it and drown or freeze to death.

silver thaw: Freezing rain that coats trees and other objects with a shell of shining, crystalline ice. A joy to gawking passengers but, because it creates dangerous road conditions, a bane to conscientious drivers.

slob ice: "Lazy" ice that does not deserve to be called ice since it not fully frozen. See also *frazil*, *lolly* and *slurry*.

slurry: A slushy form of semi-solid ice that has, not surprisingly, lent its name to the slushy, semi-solid beverage sold in large plastic cups, flavoured with synthetic saccharides and coloured with toxic pigments. See also *frazil*, *lolly* and *slob ice*.

Some people believe that a country's terrain shapes the character of its people. But what about the weather? Like Canada's climate itself, the words we use to describe (and sometimes decry) our meteorological lot in life are diverse, varied and unexpected. They reveal a resigned sense of humour and, at the same time, a respect for mighty elements beyond our control. In the final forecast, many of our most well-weathered words are, like Canadians themselves, inventive, ironic and, above all, funny.

Chapter Nine

~∞X∞~

Libation Nation

A COUNTRY OF OPPOSITES we may be, but a nation of teetotallers we are not. Not to put too fine a point on it, Canadians like their sauce. Along with commercially produced beer and wine familiar to regular imbibers, Canada also boasts its share of backroads brews and woodsy spirits. So, much like the rest of this book, the names and terms Canadians use to describe, denigrate and venerate alcohol are a mixture of folksy regionalisms and urban shorthand.

It is worth noting that Canada's two largest breweries, Molson and Labatt (although both have now been absorbed into massive multinational corporations), are a considerable source of national pride. Molson even went so far as to launch a successful ad campaign under the slogan "I AM Canadian." Part of Canadians' pride in their beer comes from the perception that Canadian beer has higher alcohol content than American beer. In some cases this is true, but as the old saying goes, "pride goeth before a fall," and hopsy *Canucks* would do well to remember that in Canada, alcohol content is calculated by volume, whereas in the U.S. it is determined by weight; this means that while the latter measurement appears lower, the alcohol content is actually the same.

At any rate, what follows will help parched readers to order the beverage that may best slake their thirst. In light of that, it seemed prudent to say a few introductory words about the names of places one can get drunk, how to describe states of drunkenness and one alleged cure for a hangover. Let us begin.

If you are in a Canadian city and looking for a place to consume some sudsy *barley beverages*, you can't do better than to determine the whereabouts of the nearest *beer parlour*. Actually, you could do quite a bit better, for not only does the phrase describe the lowest possible sort of drinking establishment (likely having chipped tile in the washrooms and plywood sheets for windows) but also, no one will know what you mean. The phrase *beer parlour* is about as up to date as a beehive hairdo. Conversely, let us suppose that you are seeking a merry tipple in the *back forty*; instead of anything so grandiose as a *beer parlour*, you are looking for a rough shed or hut where one might purchase some form of warming libation. In cases such as these, you are advised to approach the nearest *voyageur* (barring the convenient presence of a *voyageur*, just find an *inukshuk*) and inquire as to the location of the nearest *shebang*.

Once you have found some kind of local establishment, you will no doubt want to order a drink, or seven, and to this end we direct you to the following guide. Once in said establishment, unless you are a *pump sucker*, you will undoubtedly achieve some level of inebriation and will need to know how to express this happy state as clearly and coherently as your level of drunkenness permits. If you are anywhere in Canada and are simply more or less drunk, then people may refer to you as *in his/her cups*. However, if you are in a logging camp or frontier town and have attained a state of inebriation seemingly only possible by spending your entire paycheque, then you are *drunk as a thousand dollars*. If you are a male, and so drunk you are unable to perform sexually, then you have a case of *brewer's droop* (as to which many a *hockey widow* can attest). Finally, for those experiencing severe hangovers, be forewarned that if someone offers you a *prairie oyster*, it may be a beverage comprising an egg yolk suspended in brandy and alleged to be a hangover cure, or it may be a cooked bull testicle, prized as a delicacy by some, but regarded as a cure for hangovers by none.

With all of the cautionary preconditions thus stipulated, we can now proceed to the section you've all been waiting for: how to buy drinks in Canada. What follows may not be the most practical guide to ordering refreshment, but it is at least highly entertaining, and once you've had a few, you'll never remember it anyway.

Expression used in Conversation	**Literal Meaning**
Would you care for a *barley beverage/barley sandwich?*	Do you want a beer?
Are you up for a *snort* of *blackstrap?*	Do you think your constitution can withstand a shot of hearty liquor made from rum and molasses?
Can I get a *Bloody Caesar?*	Would you please concoct for me a beverage comprising vodka, Worcestershire sauce, Tabasco and Clamato juice, usually garnished with celery and served in a glass rimmed with seasoning salt?
I'll have a *Blue*.	I should like a bottle of Labatt Blue.

I'll have an *Ex*.

Would you be so good as to get me a bottle of Molson Export?

Have you ever tried a *Calgary Redeye?*

Have you ever felt inclined to swallow beer and tomato juice mixed together?

Try some of my homemade *callibogus*.

Whether you want it or not, I'm foisting this mixture of spruce beer, rum and molasses upon you.

Don't confuse *caribou* with *caribou*.

Don't mistake an antler-bearing ungulate for an alcoholic drink made from one part red wine and six parts grain alcohol.

I got a *40-pounder* for the *May two-four* weekend.

I have purchased a 40-ounce bottle of hard liquor or spirits with the intent of the consuming it on the *Victoria Day* weekend.

You're gettin' quite the *Molson muscle*.

Your beer paunch is increasing in girth.

Can I offer you a glass of *moosemilk?*

Is there anyway I could convince you to try some of my home-brewed liquor or a glass of rum and milk?

Let's get a flagon of *porch climber* for the party.

Let's get a gallon of cheap red wine in a big glass jug for the intended jollification.

This *screech* will make you screech.

This overproof rum made in Newfoundland will cause you to elicit an involuntary squeal when swallowed.

If your teeth are sensitive, you should know that this is real *snowbroth*.

If your teeth are prone to hot/cold sensitivity, I am warning you that this is very, very cold liquor.

Here, have a glass of my finest *swish*.

I insist that you have this glass of liquor made by filling an empty rum barrel with boiling water until the barrel staves have yielded their alcoholic residue.

He drank a whole *twenty-sixer* and *beulahed* everywhere.

He alone consumed an entire 26-ounce bottle of spirits and then proceeded to vomit copiously in all directions.

Can you pick me up a *two-four* when you're out?

Would you be so kind as to purchase a case of 24 bottles or cans of beer while you are out?

Chapter Ten

~∞~

Getting a Job
- or -
Goin' down the road
in the
Great White North

ALTHOUGH HISTORIANS differ on who said it first, at some point in the late 18th century, someone with a dry wit first referred to England as "a nation of shopkeepers." It is mentioned here by way of contrast, because a nation of shopkeepers Canada most definitely is not. Most people, when pondering jobs that characterize Canada, probably stray more towards the macho than the mercantile. For instance, we might be called "a nation of *lumberjacks*," "a country of *voyageurs*" or even "a state of *knuckle pickers*," but shopkeepers—most assuredly not.

Jobs in Canada are like the country itself—diverse, sometimes rugged and profoundly shaped by geography. Like anything else, the region where a job is found heavily influences both what that job is called and, in most cases, the nature of the job itself.

In the pages that follow, you will find a colourful assortment of ways to earn a buck. Some of these ancient and noble professions have gone by the wayside with the advent of mechanization, but in their names many will find a nostalgic echo of times long gone—if they ever were at all.

Let us imagine that you, a newcomer to Canada, have come to seek your fortune in our verdant forests, upon our fertile plains and amid our crashing waters (sounds like quite an adventure, doesn't it?). Upon opening the paper, your heart leaps with hope, for there before you beckon a multitude of exciting-sounding jobs. Alas, what in heaven's name do they mean? They seem to constitute a baffling selection that veers wildly between arcane specialization and superhuman endurance.

What then to make of it all? To better help you grasp the situation, we offer here a helpful primer designed to demystify the nuts and bolts of getting a job in the *Great White North*.

Exciting Opportunities in the Fur Trade

Adventure, romance, backbreaking labour

Wanted: *coureurs de bois*. Infallible tracking and orienteering skills a must. Applicants of both Aboriginal and European heritage welcome. Bilingualism an asset, but not a requirement.

If you see this, you should jump at the chance, because your prospective employers apparently possess a time machine. *Coureurs de bois* were the "runners of the woods," tough, able-bodied trappers and traders who were the backbone of Canada's early fur trade.

Seeking *voyageurs* for 10 to 14 hour workdays. Must be able to paddle at 70 strokes per minute, carry 90-lb. packs for miles on end, experience at portaging an asset. Paddles provided.

Note that because of the temporal anomalies involved, the metric system has not yet been introduced. Modern-day applicants would do well to train for a triathlon and dress for mosquitoes.

Tired of seasonal work? Do you have what it takes to be *"un vrai homme du nord"?* The successful applicant must be able to withstand severe winter temperatures. Resistance to scurvy a plus.

They're asking if you have what it takes to be a "real man of the north." This means that not only will you be a *voyageur*, but you will also work year-round, including winter. For neither the faint of heart, nor the tender of foot.

Like pork? Then sign up today to be a *mangeur de lard*. Don't worry if you're too much of a wuss to be an *homme du nord*—you can still get the summer job of a lifetime! Applicants who do not eat pork due to religious affiliation or personal preference are advised to bring their own rations.

If you're looking for *voyageur* work during the spring and summer only (perfect for students who need to earn tuition and housing costs), then you may qualify to be a "mangeur de lard" (pork eater). Be advised that you will actually be expected to eat large quantities of salted pork.

I buy your logs!

Bottom dollar paid ~ No questions asked

Beachcombers and *log pirates* can convert their new, used and second-hand logs into cash! Here at Oliver's Loggery, I pay you cash for your wood! Got some old logs up in the lumber attic? Or maybe you've recently "found" some logs on the beach (they must have just "broken free" from a logging *boom*, right?)

If you're a *beachcomber*, you scavenge beaches looking for logs that have broken loose from logging booms, then you salvage them and sell them back to the logging company. If you're a *log pirate*, then you just steal them outright and then sell them back to their rightful owners. For the work involved, these are

Well, float them on down to Oliver's Loggery and cash them in! Turn your wood into money!

probably two of the lowest paying jobs in Canada.

Attention Tillers of the Soil

Opportunities abound in the West, the Prairies and Central Canada

Come west, young people, for opportunities in *fruit ranching* await!

If watching fruit grow is your idea of excitement, this is the job for you.

Needed, general *stubble-jumpers* of any variety or expertise.

What these folks are looking for are general prairie farmers.

Urgently required: Two able-bodied individuals to fulfill the positions of *hangin' kill* and *shakin' stick*. If you actually know what these terms mean, you already have an advantage!

Now usually done by machines, *hangin' kill* refers to hanging up heavy racks of tobacco leaves to dry in a kiln, while *shakin' stick* refers to shaking them afterwards to separate the toasted tobacco leaves.

Send away now to become a *rock doctor* by correspondence.

Whether anyone will actually hire a mail-order geologist is doubtful.

Seeking fishy romance and scaly adventure?

Come to the Maritimes and jump right in! ~ An icthyophile's paradise!

Needed, someone with strong fingers and stronger stomach for *throater* position. Perks include as much free fish smell as you can carry home. If you are prone to seasickness, worry not—the *throater* is the person who stays on shore and slits the throats of the day's catch.

Do you enjoy shaking hands? Then we have the job for you—come on out and be a *shaker*. A *shaker* is someone who shakes meat out of lobster shells.

If you have a knack for precision work, then why not enjoy the fruits of an exacting career as a *knuckle picker?* Not so carefree a life as that of the *shaker*, the *knuckle-picker* picks the meat out of lobster knuckles.

If you're looking for a career that's a bit more modern, and yet still traditional, you can always become a *Mountie*. Not only will you get to embody a Canadian stereotype, but they'll also teach you to ride a horse, and you get that nifty red jacket to wear *as well*. Whether you're a boy *Mountie* or a girl *Mountie*, you can rest assured that ever since the TV program, *Due South*, *Mounties* have been regarded as *hotties* on horseback, so count your blessings that you live in a country where equine expertise and sex appeal go hand in hoof.

Finally, for those who may not be able to find steady employment (and truly, it happens to the best of us, even writers), you are still not out of options. Canada has many safeguards in place to provide when times are tough.

In the end you can always apply for *pogey*. When answering the biweekly questionnaire about your ability and diligence in looking for a job, remember that the correct answers are always—yes, yes, yes, no, yes. Bearing this simple mantra in mind will aid and comfort you as you join the ranks of what was once affectionately known as the *UIC ski team*.

Chapter Eleven

꙳❦꙳

Half-day in the Life of Canadian English
- or -
"Yes, I'm eating the red ones last. What business is it of yours?"

THERE ARE PROBABLY those among you who rightly question the dire necessity for a book like this one—and if there aren't, there should be. But just imagine the bafflement of a stranger to our land—someone who has never watched a game of hockey, who believes the *CBC* is a kind of missile, who thinks *Blue* is just a colour (psst! It's really a beer!). What would a person like this make of their first day in Canada? Submitted for your consideration is the case of a stranger in a strange land where the people use familiar words in weird ways.

You wake up in the morning on your first full day here in Canada. You've just arrived from somewhere else. Maybe it's an English-speaking country, maybe not. Really, in this case, the difference is moot. You stumble out of bed (or spring brightly to your feet depending on your bias) then go outside to explore this strange new world. In the street, you accidentally tread lightly on the foot of a passerby. It's no big deal, but before you (the foot-stepper-onner) can apologize, the passerby (the foot-step-onnee) turns to you and says "*Sorry*" and walks cheerily down the street. What gives? The person whose foot you just stepped on has **apologized to you**! Strange customs here.

You decide that you need to drink some coffee to sharpen your senses, and you reach into your pocket for the Canadian currency you prudently acquired before travelling. You pull out a handful of brightly coloured bank notes and what look like large gold coins; it seems to be a mixture of play money and pirate treasure; what a mad house this country is! You ask a passerby where the nearest place to get a coffee is, and they reply, "There's a *Tim's* on the corner, *eh*?" Okay, it seems you are looking for an establishment called "Atim's," although the "*eh*" makes you wonder if the passerby was actually asking **you** for directions.

You start walking towards the corner. On the way, you pass a small art gallery with a sign that says "*Group of Seven* prints on sale now." *Group of Seven*? They must be political dissidents. And presumably they are allowed to raise money for their own defense by painting and selling pictures. What an enlightened society you have chanced upon!

At last, you reach the corner and see that the coffee emporium is actually called *Tim's*. Ah, well, at least that makes sense. You enter and politely ask for a medium coffee with two creams and two sugars. "Right," says the clerk, "*double-double.*" This strikes you as odd since you're pretty sure that you actually said, "Two creams and two sugars." You decide to hold your tongue, however, because the customs here are unfamiliar to you. You proffer your funny money and receive your change. Then the coffee comes, and it is delicious, obviously having two creams and two sugars as you had requested. Clearly the term *double-double* is some sort of local nomenclature, a lingua franca, as it were, of these strange people among whom you now find yourself sipping tasty, albeit, oddly named coffee.

Heartened by the excellent coffee, you decide to buy a confection of some kind and settle upon a rattling box of something called *Smarties*. You sit down at a table and open the box of *Smarties*, which prove to be small, brightly coloured choking hazards with a crunchy candy coating and a soft chocolate centre. You marvel at the myriad colours. Being an orderly soul, you decide to eat them in order of colour. Which ones to save for last? Perhaps the red. Just as you have arrived at this silent decision, a middle-aged adult at the next table leans over and asks with a twinkling eye, *"When you eat your Smarties, do you eat the red ones last?"* Are these people clairvoyant, nosey or both? Frustrated at this invasion of your privacy, you say, "Yes, I'm eating the red ones last. What business is it of yours?" The interloper seems taken aback, possibly even hurt, and sits back with a hurried, *"Sorry."* Hmm, there it is again—*Sorry*—only this time it made sense.

Enough time passes that you have actually started in on the red *Smarties*, all the while watching the people pass by the window. They seem friendly enough, and yet their strange ways and even stranger language are clearly going to require careful navigation. If only there were some sort of book to which you could refer, maybe a *Primer of Canadian English*, or perhaps a *Lexicon of the North*, even a *Dictionary of Canadianisms*. O' for such a book as this...

PART TWO

A Canadian Lexicon

~⋊⋉~

A - Zed

ABM

Short for Automated Bank Machine. Upon hearing *ABM*, security-minded Americans of a certain age think "Anti Ballistic Missile Shield," because in the U.S., people exclusively call *bank machines* ATMs.

"Excuse me, is there an *ABM* around here?"

"Why, are we under attack? Have you called Homeland Security?"

Acadia

A name used to describe a geographical region and a culture, both heavily influenced by early French settlers. Historically, the name *Acadia* referred to a French colony that included all of Canada's Maritime provinces as well as parts of Québec and New England. Today, *Acadia* connotes the present-day, French-speaking culture throughout the maritime region, especially with reference to cuisine and folk culture. During the 1960s, proposals were afoot to amalgamate the provinces into a single entity, to be known as *Acadia*. (Other proposed names included, embarrassingly, Maritopia, Atlantica and, confusingly, New England.)

Adanac

"Canada" spelled backwards and, as such, a popular name for small businesses. Look in the telephone directory of any large Canadian city to find *Adanac* Contractors, *Adanac* Shipping, AAA *Adanac* Aardvark Aquariums Associated, and so on.

(L')affaire est ketchup

"Everything's okay," in some French Canadian dialects.

"Comment ça va, mon ami?" (How are things, my friend?)

"*L'affaire est ketchup.*"

aft

Informal, short for "afternoon." Overheard at a Canadian high school:

"What do you have this *aft*?"

"Got a *spare*."

"So do I. Wanna drink a *two-four*, then go *smoke up*?"

"Just don't *beulah* in my car."

after

In Newfoundland idiom, *after* is used when someone has just completed a deed or action. "You've already driven into the ditch; you're *after* makin' a mistake." OR "You're *after* tryin' three months to get her to take you back." OR "How many times am I *after* tellin' you, it's the green side of the sod you're layin' as faces upwards."

airsome

Cold, fresh or bracing weather, especially in New-foundland. "'Tis an *airsome* day this mornin'."

aksunai

An Inuit word meaning "be strong" and often used in greeting or farewell. "*Aksunai, kabluna.*"

Alberta Clipper

A cold wind reaching speeds of nearly 100 kilo-metres per hour, often used disparagingly in the U.S. mid-west, but usually with pride at home: "Windy enough for you?" "Yup, it's a real *Alberta Clipper* today."

AlCan

The former name of the firm "Rio Tinto Alcan" and short for "Aluminum Company of Canada." From 1925 onward, this aluminum producer was known under variants of this name and its trian-gular, stylized "A" logo was familiar to consumers from any number of products, including alumi-num foil baking platters and ash-trays. In 2007, *AlCan*'s own subsidiary, "Rio Tinto," orchestrated a friendly takeover, and the company's name became "Rio Tinto AlCan."

all dressed

1) A popular flavour of potato chip not available, nor often heard of, in the U.S. 2) In Québec, New Brunswick and eastern Ontario, a way of request-ing every available garnish (typically ketchup,

81

mustard, relish, lettuce, onion and tomato) when ordering an item such as a hamburger in a restaurant.

all kinds

An informal expression meaning "abundant, but non-specific." "Sure, come on over. We got *all kinds* of work for you to do." OR "Look, *kabluna*, if you *beulah* on my *mukluks* you'll be in *all kinds* of trouble."

all over the pond

In PEI, confusion or disorientation, usually due to drunkenness.

"*Sorry* that I peed in your *ice hole*."

"Whose *ice hole* did you **mean** to pee in?"

"Uh...mine, I guess."

"You're *all over the pond* tonight."

alouette

French for "skylark," this word means many different things to Canadians. 1) The name of a popular French language folk song about plucking a skylark prior to cooking and eating it. 2) The first Canadian-built satellite launched in 1962. 3) The name of the Canadian Football League's Montréal team (although the current franchise is actually the former Baltimore Stallions).

angakok

An Inuit medicine man or shaman. The local *anga-kok* may be seen not only as a healer, but also as holding sway over successful hunting and fishing ventures.

anglais

French for "English" and used by *francophones* to describe both the language and culture of *anglophones*. Even Canadians who stopped taking French in Grade 11 know what this means.
"Parlez vous *anglais?*" (Do you speak English?)
"Oui, je parle *anglais.*" (Yes, I speak English.)

anglo/anglophone

An informal French Canadian term to describe English-speaking Canadians, especially those living in Québec. Usually its tone is matter of fact, but it can also be used as an insult.
"Parlez vous *anglais?*" (Do you speak English?)
"*Vas pèter dans le trèfle, anglo!*" (Go fart in the clover, English-speaking Canadian!)

Anne of Green Gables

A famous and beloved character created by Lucy Maud Montgomery (1874–1942), first appearing in an eponymous novel in 1908 and thereafter in several sequels. Her full name is Anne Shirley, and in the first book she is an 11-year-old orphan with red hair and freckles who is mistakenly sent to live with a middle-aged couple in rural PEI. She is strong willed and adventurous, soon getting into many scrapes and adventures in her new town. Over the next several books, Anne grows up into a middle-aged adult herself. Aside from potatoes, *Anne of Green Gables* is probably PEI's most famous and lucrative export, having spawned films, TV shows, plays and additional books by writers other than L.M. Montgomery. While she has fan clubs all over the world, Anne is particularly popular in Japan in much the same way that Jerry Lewis is mysteriously popular in France.

any-sex season
This rarely heard hunting term refers to an open season when it is legal to shoot either male or female moose or deer. However, for thousands of Canadian university students, it could just as easily refer to *Reading Week*.

apass/apast
In Newfoundland, a folksy way to describe going past a place or landmark: "I was *after* drivin' my truck *apass* the end of the dock, so I knew I was in *all kinds* of trouble." OR it may refer to a point in time that has passed: "It was *apast* my birthday that I swore never to drink *screech* again."

apathetic
A state of being indifferent to either opinion or circumstance, often ascribed to Canadians as a group during the 1970s and '80s. "People say that Canadians are *apathetic*, but we really don't care."

Arborite
A brand name for the hard, thin surface that covers particleboard desks, countertops and other furni-

ture. The Arborite Company was founded in 1948 in Cornwall, Ontario, but the term has come into general use to describe any similar product. Overheard in a U.S. hardware store where a Canadian was shopping:

"Where are the *Arborite* counter tops?"

"You mean Formica?"

"No, I mean *Arborite.*"

"We only have Formica."

"Look, all I want is a melamine laminate of some kind."

"Right—we have Formica."

arg

Short for "argue" in the Newfoundland of yore. "Don't *arg* with me *my son*, or you'll get naught but *bare-legged* tea for *tea.*"

armstrong method

West Coast slang for anything done by manual labour instead of machine or mechanism. "*Skidder's* broken. We'll have to shift this load of *pecker poles* with the *armstrong method.*"

as well

An alternative way of saying "also" more likely to be used by Canadians than other English speakers, especially at the beginning of a sentence. "*As well*, Canadians call couches *chesterfields*, soda *pop* and candy bars *chocolate bars.*"

assist

An otherwise useful word whose meaning has now been bastardized by hockey players to mean points awarded to the last one or two players whose sticks touch the puck before the scorer's.

(l')Assomption sash

A long, brightly coloured sash of the kind pictured in most depictions of *voyageurs*, usually wrapped around their waists, but sometimes also looped from one shoulder to the opposing hip. The sashes were about four to six inches wide, eight to ten feet long and interwoven with colourful patterns, the most famous being the zig-zaggy "arrow" design that resembles cartoon lightning bolts. The best of them were made in l'Assomption, Québec, and sashes were widely distributed as trade goods by fur trading companies.

Atlantic Canada

The provinces of Nova Scotia, New Brunswick, PEI and Newfoundland. This term is often used and understood to be interchangeable with *Maritimes*, although technically the latter does not include Newfoundland.

August long weekend

A *civic holiday* observed on the first Monday in August except in Québec and PEI. "We're going camping for the *August long weekend*."

autoroute

An expressway, so-called in Québec and, as such, a term of puzzlement when read by Americans on road maps. Overheard at a Montréal gas station:

"Whut's this *autoroute* thang here on the map."

"It is an expressway, monsieur."

"Then why don't you call it an expressway?"

"Because we call it an *autoroute*, monsieur."

"Different strokes for different folks I guess. Now how much of this *funny money* do I owe you for the gas?"

Avro Arrow

A supersonic jet fighter developed in the late 1950s by Avro Aircraft Limited based in Malton, Ontario. Abruptly cancelled in 1959, the project remains one of the great "what-ifs" in Canadian history with implications for national defense, air superiority and national sovereignty.

ayaya

Inuit singing that uses the sounds "ayaya" instead of actual words.

B

baby bonus

An informal name for the Family Allowance, a government stipend for families with children under the age of 16. Introduced in 1948, the *baby bonus* is widely seen as the narrow end of the wedge in the eventual adoption of Canada's social security programs, including universal healthcare and *UI* (see employment insurance).

Baby Duck

One of Canada's fledgling (pun intended) domestic wines made by Bright's winery. Fermented from grapes that were not considered good enough for a dry table wine, *Baby Duck* was fizzy and sweet. At its peak in 1973 it sold eight million bottles. In spite of its popularity, by the end of the decade it had become rather déclassé, possibly because the general wine-drinking public had developed a more collectively refined palate. Still available, in perception and social status it can be seen as a cousin of the German wine, Blue Nun.

"Is this fizzy water and grape juice with some alcohol thrown in?"

"Sort of. It's called *Baby Duck*."

back bacon

1) In its strictest sense, *back bacon* (a.k.a. *Canadian bacon*) is a leaner cut of pork loin than the streaky, fatty bacon usually served in Canada and the U.S. However, general confusion on both sides of the border has resulted in a second accepted meaning; that is, 2) *Peameal bacon*, rashers of bacon, the outer edges of which are coated in peameal. For an entire generation of Canadians, *back bacon* became a household word when the *McKenzie Brothers* famously recorded a version of "The Twelve Days of Christmas," in which, on the fourth day, the gift was "four pounds of back bacon." All that being said, most Canadians eat "American" bacon.

back door trots

In PEI, diarrhea, so-called because of the need to run out the back door to get to the outhouse in time.

"What did he have for breakfast?"

"*Scrod* and *screech*."

"That's a recipe for the *back door trots* if ever there was one."

back forty

Literally, the 40 acres of a large farm or ranch farthest away from farm house and barn. Figuratively, a remote area devoid of regular human inhabitants, such as might be favoured for camping.

B

"What you doin' for *May two-four?*"
"Packin' up our tent and hittin' the *back forty*."

Baise-moué l'ail (Kiss my garlic)

A French Canadian insult along the lines of "Kiss my ass," but for some obscure reason substituting garlic for buttocks. An exchange between two *anglos* practicing insults for their trip to Québec might go:

"*Ferme ton gorlot!*"
"Oh yeah? Well, *Baise-moué l'ail!*"

bakeapple

An edible member of the raspberry family having an amber fruit. Apparently this name comes from the *Big Eyebrows'* inability to pronounce the Inuktitut word, "appik" for "apple."

"What did the *kabluna* just say?"
"I think he said, '*bakeapple*'?"
"Instead of appik?"
"Yup."
"You realize that these people are completely clueless, right? And we're going to have to help them not to freeze to death during the winter."
"Why?"

baker's fog

In Atlantic Canada, store-bought bread was once (and may still be) disparagingly called *baker's fog* because, compared to hearty home-made bread, it is fluffy and insubstantial—like fog. "I've had a whole loaf of this *baker's fog* and I'm still hungry!"

ball hockey

1) A hockey game played indoors with plastic sticks and a hard plastic ball. 2) A hockey game played outside in the street with regular sticks and a tennis ball.

ballicatter

In Atlantic Canada, a rugged and irregular bank of ice formed along the shore by the freezing tides. It may be a mispronunciation of "barricade" (possibly due to the speaker's lips being frozen together by the same cold that froze the surf in the first place).

"He's such a *bostoon* that he can't even tell the difference between *frazil* and *ballicatter.*"

"D'ye need me to pour some boiling water on your lips to thaw them apart?"

band

An administrative unit of First Nations government still often but incorrectly called an Indian band. Bands are recognized by the federal government.

bang the bush

An old Haligonian expression meaning "to surpass everything" and sure to elicit consternation when used in polite company.

"Well, if your Limoge porcelain don't just *bang the bush!*"

"I beg your pardon, sir!"

"You won't be servin' *bare-legged* in that!"

B

bangbelly

A dense Newfoundland dessert cake comprising cooked rice, flour, molasses, raisins, salt pork and spices.

"Care for a bit of *bangbelly*?"

"Er...maybe a *Coffee Crisp* instead—it's a nice light snack."

bank machine

An everyday Canadian term for what Americans commonly call an ATM (for Automated Teller Machine, a term Canadians use as well, but not exclusively). Overheard in a U.S. city:

"Excuse me, is there a *bank machine* around here?"

"You mean an ATM?"

"Isn't that what I said?"

"You said *bank machine*."

"Also known as an ATM."

"Then why didn't you just say ATM?"

bannock

Heavy bread made from flour, water, fat and salt. Bannock is generally perceived as being a "wilderness" staple, not only eaten in sometimes-impoverished Aboriginal communities but also consumed on the trail by the likes of trappers and dog sledding explorers.

"Why have you packed a brick wrapped in bread dough in your duffle bag?"

"It's *bannock*."

"Is it to feed the dogs with?"

"No, it's for us."

"Well, that's good, because the dogs won't eat it."

B

bannock puncher

A bachelor who can cook a bit, so-called at the turn of the 20th century in the Prairies. Overheard between two women in olden-days Alberta:

"Klondike Bill cooked supper for me the other night and, you know, the flames weren't nearly as high as I'd feared."

"He's become quite the *bannock puncher* since he took that correspondence course on how to boil water without burning it."

banquet burger

A hamburger with bacon and cheese. This is one of those phrases sure to cause friction between Canadians and Americans. For instance, an American who enters a Canadian restaurant and orders a "bacon-cheeseburger" will be understood. However, a Canadian in the U.S. who orders an exotic sounding (read "probably foreign and therefore dangerous") *banquet burger* is likely to raise suspicion—after all, aren't thim thar Canadians part French or somethin'?

baptême

A *sacré* that references baptism in the Roman Catholic tradition.

B

bare-legged

In Newfoundland, descriptive of black tea offered without food.

"The cupboard's empty, but I can use my *hot arse* to brew you a cup of *bare-legged* tea."

"And I'll be grateful for that, *my son.*"

bargoon

A bargain. This is a Canadianism? Really? Don't Americans say this too?

"Hey, I got this Canadian dictionary at 90 percent off the cover price."

"What a *bargoon.*"

"See, I'm American and I know what that means."

"I thought you would."

barley beverage

Beer. "Would you like a *barley beverage?*"

barley sandwich

Beer. As the previous entry suggests, all you have to do is take the word "barley" and shove it before an otherwise innocent noun such as "beverage," "sandwich" or "pop" (not "soda") and you have a phrase that any Canadian who isn't a *pump sucker* will happily identify as one that promises beer.

bateau

French for "boat," but here referring specifically to a flat-bottomed vessel about 30 feet

B

long and propelled either by sails or oars. Bateaux were used by fur traders, merchants and, notably, Bill Johnston, the so-called Pirate of the Thousand Islands.

bathtub race

Every year, on the last weekend in July, Nanaimo, BC, hosts a race in which contestants brave the ocean waters in motorized boats built from bath-tubs (you can't make this stuff up). When the tra-dition started in 1967, the race started in Nanaimo and ended at Kitsilano Beach in Vancouver. Since the mid-1990s though, the route has been from Nanaimo to nearby Departure Bay. Now, as well as lending its name to delicious *Nanaimo bars*, Nanaimo is recognized as the Official Bathtub Race Capital of the World, with all the attendant rights and privileges conferred upon it by whoever makes this stuff up.

Bavarian cream

In Ontario, a kind of *doughnut* with chocolate on top and an edible petroleum product instead of whipped cream or custard in the middle (see also *bismarck*, Manitoba definition).

bay girl/bayman/bay noddy

In Atlantic Canada, an inhabitant of the *outports*. Depending on context, the term may connote affection, disdain or pride. It may also suggest homespun common sense mixed with coastal whimsy. Sometimes it suggests all of the above at

the same time.
"You appear to be stirring your tea with a fork."
"I couldn't find a spoon."
"Are you by any chance a *bayman*?"
"That's *bay noddy* to you and proud of it!"

BC Bud

Potent marijuana grown in BC and thusly named because the "buds" of the pot plant are the part most commonly smoked.
"This is some fine *BC Bud*, my friend."
"Are you hungry at all?"
"I've got a plate of *Nanaimo bars* here."
"Got any potato chips?"
"*Ketchup,* Dill or *All Dressed*?"

beachcombers

People who prowl beaches looking for potentially useful or profitable items washed up on shore. Originally it referred to people who salvaged and sold logs that had broken away from log *booms* and washed up on the beach. "The Beachcombers" was also the name of an inexplicably popular and bafflingly long-lived *CBC* television program about—surprise, surprise—people who salvaged and sold logs that had broken away from log *booms* and washed up on the beach. It ran (and ran and ran) from 1972 to 1990, making it the longest running dramatic series on Canadian TV.
"Wanna watch *Beachcombers?*"
"God, is that show **still** on?"

beauty (pron: bew-TEE)

1) An exclamation meaning that circumstances are good, a task has been well done or both. "You just won the lottery? *Beauty!*" 2) An adjective meaning good or excellent. "You've got a real *beauty* car!" or "*Take off,* it's a *beauty* way to go."

B

beaver

(castor canadensis). Our national symbol, appearing on the obverse of the Canadian nickel and lending its name and buck-toothed likeness to any number of Canadian enterprises and products. Look in your local Yellow Pages for names like *Beaver* Café, *Beaver* Chemicals, *Beaver* Window & Awning, and so on.

Beaver tail

A proprietary dessert consisting of a flattened, fried pastry about 30 centimetres long and 8 centimetres wide, a shape that discerning readers will recognize as resembling a beaver's tail. It is typically garnished with sugar, cinnamon and/or maple syrup, though savoury toppings can be added as well. Invented in Ottawa by Grant and Pam Hooker, this most Canadian of desserts is now licensed worldwide.

beer parlour

A deceptively genteel name for what is otherwise the lowest, toughest sort of bar.

"Goodness gracious, a *beer parlour!* That sounds pleasant."

"It may sound pleasant, but you can bet it won't smell pleasant."

bellcast

A traditional architectural style popular in Québec and characterized by roofs shaped like squared-off bells.

(la) belle province

A common nickname for Québec, meaning "the beautiful province."

"We're honeymooning in *la belle province.*"

bench-clearing brawl

An infrequent but highly anticipated hockey fight in which all of the players from both teams, those on the ice and those on the benches, throw off their gloves, swarm onto the ice and start pummelling each other because they are such good sportsmen.

Beothuk

An extinct Aboriginal tribe who inhabited Newfoundland.

better than a slap on the belly with a dead fish

A humorous way of commenting on circumstances ranging from moderately good to quite excellent.

"We want to hire you to write a book on how to speak Canadian."

"Well, that's *better than a slap on the belly with a dead fish.*"

beulah
Although it sounds like the name of someone's bingo-playing maiden aunt, in PEI and a few other places, *beulah* means "to vomit."
"He drank a whole *forty pounder* and then *beula-hed* up all over my car."

beurre d'arachide
French for "peanut butter." *Beurre d'arachide* is included here because it is one of many French terms recognized by even the most die-hard *anglos* since they see it constantly on product packaging. English-only speakers may even use it humorously: "Don't forget to pick up some *beurre d'arachide.*"

Big Eyebrow
The English equivalent of the Inuktitut word, *kabluna,* used to describe white European explorers and traders. Generally used either matter-of-factly or as a term of contempt.
"That *Big Eyebrow* is really getting on my nerves."
"Go pee in his *ice hole.*"

Big Nickel
A 9-metre (30-foot) tall replica of a 1951 Canadian nickel located in Sudbury, Ontario. Although it was begun in 1963 and completed in 1964,

B

instigator Ted Szilva modelled it on the 1951 coin because there had been a special minting that year to celebrate the bicentennial of nickel's chemical isolation. In turn, nickel mining was (and still is) one of Sudbury's key industries. As with the actual nickel its design is based on, one side of the *Big Nickel* shows King George VI, and the other, a smelting refinery with a large central smokestack (no beaver, for those who may be wondering).

"Is the *Big Nickel* one of the *giants of the Prairies?*"

"Well, no. To begin with, I don't know anyone who would describe Sudbury as the Prairies."

Big Perogie

One of the *giants of the Prairies*, the *Big Perogie*, is a 7.6-metre (25-foot) tall sculpture of a giant perogie impaled by an equally giant fork. It looms over the town of Glendon, Alberta.

"Is that supposed to be a giant pizza pocket?"

"That's the *Big Perogie*. You're not from around here, are ya?"

big time

In the Maritimes, a party or occasion.

"You should come on over—we'll be havin' a real *big time* tonight."

bill

A written tabulation of money owed for a meal in a restaurant. This entry is included for the benefit of Americans travelling north of the 49th parallel, because such a reckoning *south of the border* is called the "check" (Note: not *cheque*).

bismarck

1) In Alberta or Saskatchewan, a sugar-coated *doughnut* filled with jam (see also *jelly doughnut*).
2) In Manitoba, a chocolate-glazed *doughnut* with a cream filling (see also *Bavarian cream*). Overheard in Ontario coffee shop:

"Hi, I'm from Alberta or Saskatchewan. Do you have any *bismarcks?*"

"What's a *bismarck?*"

"Why, it's a sugar-coated *doughnut* filled with jam."

"A *jelly doughnut?*"

"I guess so. Oh, that's my friend there coming in from parking the car. He'll want something, too."

"Hi, I'm from Manitoba. Do you have any *bismarcks?*"

bivouac

An overnight or temporary camp without tents, typically pitched by rugged (and presumably handsome) explorers of wild frontier colonies like Canada.

"My, but you're a rugged and handsome explorer. What say we do some nighttime exploring at your place?"

"Er...my place is actually a *bivouac* about half-way up that mountain there."

"Maybe my place then—I've got a floor **and** a roof."

"And I've got a wineskin full of *blackstrap*."

"It's a date."

blackstrap

Hearty liquor made from rum and molasses. Overheard the morning after a night of black-strapping:

"Why am I waking up here at your *bivouac?* I thought we were going to my place."

"We did. That was where we drank all the *black-strap* and then I carried you up the mountain."

blanket toss

An Inuit pastime in which a circle of people all grasp the edge of a large round blanket or canvas and combine their strength to toss one of their number into the air; it's kind of like a co-operative trampoline.

blatherskite

An informal term meaning a speaker of non-sense, for some reason preferred by Members of Parliament.

"The Honourable Member's reputation as a *blatherskite* precedes him."

bleacher

1) A fair-complexioned woman. 2) A young, unmarried woman but one who is definitely "marriageable."

"Susan White is outta sight."

"Yeah, she's a real *bleacher.*"

"That Liza's okay, too."

"Yup, she's a real *dilsey.* Smells a bit like fish though." (See also *I'se the By.*)

block parent

Volunteer households in suburban communities where children in need of help can go in case of emergency. Typically a red and white sign is put up in one window.

Bloody Caesar

A mixed alcoholic cocktail made from vodka, Worcestershire sauce, Tabasco and *Clamato juice,* usually garnished with celery and served in a glass rimmed with seasoning salt. *South of the border,* it's a Bloody Mary, and has plain tomato juice instead of *Clamato juice.* The *Bloody Caesar* was invented in Calgary during the late 1960s. Walter Chell, a restaurant bartender, was on the lookout out for a cocktail that would complement the Italian food his establishment served. He toiled away, looking for the right combination, until he squeezed some clam juice into a Bloody Mary and so was born the new cocktail that all his patrons said was "fit for an emperor," hence its august name.

Blue

Universally understood verbal shorthand for "Labatt Blue," the flagship beer of Labatt breweries. "Can I have a *Blue,* please?"

blue box

A blue plastic box used to contain recyclable items until they can be picked up by the recycling truck or otherwise conveyed to a recycling depot.

blueberry grunt

A Maritime dessert of cooked blueberries with a dumpling-like topping. The name may come from the sound made by the concoction as it boils away in the saucepan.

"Can ye hear that *blueberry grunt?*"

"Look, if the blueberry's grunting, let's leave it alone."

blueberry run

In PEI, 1) A heavy rain that washes away ripe blueberries. 2) Diarrhea from eating blueberries. While you should exercise caution when leaving the house during either instance, in rare cases it really doesn't matter which way you use it:

"A *blueberry run* sure is good for the crops."

Bluenose

1) A nickname for Nova Scotians. 2) A race-winning sailing ship that appears on the Canadian dime. No one really knows why Nova Scotians are so-called, but some possibilities are that cold, wet weather makes fishermen's noses turn blue; a nose-shaped species of potato grown in Nova Scotia may have sprouted a blue tip; or, least likely, but most excitingly, a Nova Scotia privateer during the War of 1812 had a blue-painted

cannon mounted in the bow and so earned the name *Bluenose*.

bluff(y)

1) In the Prairies, a grove of trees surrounding a sunken creek or slough. 2) Minus the "y," in the rest of Canada, a cliff or embankment, often with trees at the bottom.

boil-up

Teatime in the wilderness, either on the trail or in camp. More often called *mug-up*.

Bombardier

The eponymous inventor of a covered snowmobile that evolved into the *ski-doo* as we know it today. Pronounced "Bom-ba-DEER," the term first referred specifically to Bombardier's invention but eventually came to refer any motorized *snow machine*.

boneyize

An obscure expression reportedly used by kids on the Prairies and meaning, more or less, "dibs"; that is, "I claim it for myself!" Its usage is not clear, but presumably might have been spoken thus:
"Oh, look—an oil patch."
"*Boneyize!*"

book off

To schedule one's self off from work or any other daily obligation. Again, doesn't everyone say this?

B

The sources consulted for this book would have us believe otherwise.

"I've *booked off* work for the afternoon. Wanna go watch the *submarine races?*"

"You realize I **am** your boss?"

"Oh, that's not a problem. I'm very broad-minded."

boom

A floating enclosure made of logs, joined by chains. Booms are used in the lumber industry as floating corrals for logs and pulpwood. They may be stationary or towed behind tugboats to transport logs from one area to another.

bostoon

A clumsy, stupid fellow so-called in Newfoundland.

"Did I tell you that my brother-in-law managed to get his tongue stuck to a *clumper?*"

"*Brewis* for brains, that one."

"Yup, a real *bostoon.*"

boughten

A disparaging adjective used by prairie homesteaders to describe store-bought bread inferior to the homemade variety. "This *boughten* bread is rotten."

Boxing Week

The week between Christmas and New Year's Day, characterized in Canada by a weeklong orgy of 50-percent-off sales for items, including stereo equipment, appliances, fur coats as well as other, more everyday consumer articles.

boy/by

In Newfoundland, an informal way to address a male of any age, except your own father. Usually pronounced "by," it is so well known across Canada as to border on stereotype. If you are not actually in Newfoundland, injecting the word *by* into a conversation is excellent shorthand to connote proximity to or familiarity with the East Coast, usually sarcastically. However, for Newfoundlanders, it is simply an everyday form of address: "How are ye, *by?*" (See also *I'se the by*)

brain bucket

In hockey parlance, a helmet worn during play to protect the cranium.

"Did he just score on his own net?"

"Yup. He really should have started wearing the old *brain bucket* earlier in his career."

brasserie

In Québec, a pub or bar (from the French for "brewery"). Very occasionally this term confuses Anglo and American women who read the signs and assume that they can purchase brassieres and other unmentionables within.

"Oh, that's nice, dear. At **this** *brasserie*, you can sit and have a drink while I'm in the fitting room. It's just like the laundromats back home."

B

brewer's droop

Impotence due to drink.

"I hate *playoff* season—it means more *brewer's droop* than you can shake a stick at."

brewis

A hearty and beloved Newfoundland stew made from bread or biscuit boiled in fatty broth. Pronounced "brooze," it is sometimes eaten for breakfast along with cod in much the same way that baked beans are eaten with breakfast elsewhere. For some Newfoundlanders it is, simply put, comfort food. "It's a *mauzy* day out there. Let's have *brewis* with breakfast."

brewski

Slang for "beer." "Care for a *brewski?*"

brouhaha

A large hockey fight, but not quite a *bench-clearing brawl*. Overheard between two hockey commentators:

"Would you say we're seeing a *bench-clearing brawl*, Don?"

"Obviously not, Ron, because the benches aren't clear. Right now it's a donnybrook, that **could** turn into a *bench-clearing brawl*."

"I suppose you could call it a mélée."

"Or a major altercation."

"You know, I think at this point we're safe in upgrading it to a *brouhaha*."

B

browner

1) Short for "brown noser"; that is, someone whose nose is brown from kissing the backsides of their superiors so frequently and so deeply: "Every morning he goes to *Tim's* to get the boss' coffee for him—what a *browner!*" 2) In Ontario public schools, a good student, regardless of whether the pupil is a backside-kisser or not. "You got a hundred percent on the test?! You're a *browner*."

buffalo jump

Any steep cliff where Plains Indians (especially the Blackfoot) stampeded buffalo over the edge for the purposes of skinning and eating them. The most famous is Head-Smashed-In *Buffalo Jump* near Fort Macleod, Alberta. Used from approximately 4000 BC until the late 19th century, the buffalo bone deposits are 10 metres (30 feet) deep in places. It is also the site of a museum and interpretive centre about Blackfoot culture.

buggerlugs

A friendly insult shared between the old-timers in PEI and rarely heard nowadays. "Look at old *buggerlugs* drivin' by in his scrap heap."

bull of the woods

A logging term of yore to describe the best or toughest logger. In logging camps it was an informal name for the head man. Now it is used more as an appellation for winners of *logging bees* and related contests. "And *Whistle Punk* Pete takes this year's *Bull of the Woods* title for placing first in the 'Shaving with an Axe' competition."

bull puncher

Old logging slang for the person who drove the horse-pulled cart or sled full of logs.

bullamarue

In Newfoundland, a loud aggressive person or show-off.

"When he was a kid, he'd win at *steppycock,* hoppin' on one foot and all the while singin' *I'se the By* and well at that."

"What a *bullamarue.*"

bum

Informal for buttocks. Canadians get this from our British background and admittedly Americans also use it to mean the same thing but much less frequently. More often in the U.S. it is used to describe a tramp, homeless person or, as Canadians would say, a *rubby.*

bumbleberry

A mixture of berries such as blackberries, raspberries, blueberries, strawberries and so forth. It appears most often as a pie filling but is also encountered in jams and yogourt.

bumper shining

An winter activity so-named in Manitoba and

B

Saskatchewan but practiced all across Canada by children and adolescents to the utter horror of their parents. Being careful to stay in the driver's blind spot, *bumper shiners* grasp the rear bumper of a truck in icy weather to be dragged along for a ride. Imagine water skiing without the water or the skis.

bumwad
Slang for toilet paper. Also an insult of utter contempt.
"Don't listen to anything this *bumwad* says."

bunch-quitter
Western slang for a horse that has the habit of straying from the herd.

bunny hug
What the rest of the world calls a "hoodie," apparently people in Saskatchewan call a *bunny hug*. Either way, it's still a long-sleeved, hooded pullover with a low-slung pocket at the front. It's difficult to imagine gangsta rap having quite the same impact without the word "hoodie."
"Yo yo, my homeys in they *bunny hugs* gonna pop a cap in yo ass."

bush pilot
A pilot who flies small aircraft and delivers mail, medicine and consumer goods to remote northern communities.

B

bush salmon

In parts of BC, slang for poached deer.

butter tart

A delicious gooey snack consisting of a mixture of butter, eggs, brown sugar and raisins, all contained in a tart shell about the size of a hockey puck. Some think the recipe migrated from a town in Scotland called Ecclefechan, while others note a suspicious similarity between the flavour of butter tarts and that of pecan pie filling, popular in the U.S. (where presumably, they don't have butter tarts). If you're planning to compare, make sure you have at least 20 litres of milk on standby, for it's going to be thirsty work.

by times/betimes

PEI slang for "occasionally."

"Marge's husband only works *by times*."

"I think 'seasonal' is what he prefers to call it."

cabane à sucre
French Canadian for *sugar shack*.

caf
Slang for "cafeteria," especially in high schools and universities.
"I've got a *spare* this *aft*. What about you?"
"I'll meet you in the *caf*."

caisse populaire
In Québec and *francophone* communities across Canada, this term refers to a financial savings and loan institution similar to a credit union.

Calgary Redeye
A mixture of beer and tomato juice, amazingly meant to be drunk by humans.
"Care for a *Calgary Redeye*?"
"*Lorsh*, no. I'd rather have *callibogus*."

Calgary Stampede
A massive 10-day festival that takes place annually in Calgary from early to mid-July. There are rodeo demonstrations, parades, *First Nations* exhibits, concerts, chuck wagon races and (for some reason) pancake breakfasts.

câlice

A *sacré* referencing the chalice used in receiving sacramental wine.

callibogus

A concoction intended for drinking, made from spruce beer, rum and molasses. One might expect this delicacy to bear the warning: FOR EXTERNAL USE ONLY, but apparently in Newfoundland they actually willingly swallow the stuff— further (and probably over-) proof that Newfoundlanders are simply tougher than the rest of us.

"Care for a *Calgary Redeye?*"

"*Lorsh*, no. I'd rather have *callibogus.*"

camp

1) In Northern Ontario and parts of the Maritimes, a summerhouse or cottage. "You call this *camp?* Good Lord, it's nicer than my house." 2) A secondary parcel of land with either camping grounds or rough shelters located close to a cottage or summerhouse. "Ah, see? A firepit, some tents and a cooler full of beer—now **this** is a *camp.*"

Can you get outside of all that?

A pleasing expression meaning, "Can you eat all that?" Contrary to some cultures, in which eating everything on your plate is considered poor manners because it suggests your host hasn't given you enough, here in North America, we like our food and we don't care who knows it. It's understood that long harsh winters require

lots of sustenance—why be coy about it?
"Here's your *lumberjack breakfast. Can you get out-side of all that?"*

Canada
The name of our nation, seemingly derived from the Iroquoian word *kanata,* for "village" or "community."

Canada Day
A public holiday celebrating confederation (the advent of Canada's nationhood) on July 1, 1867. It is generally observed on July 1 unless that day falls on a Sunday, in which case the holiday is taken on July 2. It also coincides with *moving day* in Québec.

Canada Dry (a.k.a. "The Champagne of Ginger Ales," followed by a heavenly chorus of voices singing *Canada Dry*)
An internationally famous brand of ginger ale invented in 1904 by Toronto chemist and pharmacist John J. McGlaughlin.

Canadarm
A giant robotic arm designed and built in Canada for use in NASA's space shuttle program. With an overall length of 15 metres (50 feet), the *Canadarm* has a "shoulder," "elbow" and "wrist." Among other things, it is used for deploying, positioning and repairing satellites as well as serving as a secure tether for astronauts working outside of the space

shuttle. Although a total of five arms have been built, they are collectively referred to as "the" *Canadarm,* as if there were only one. Pronunciation should be "CA-na-darm," but some pronounce it as two separate words: Canada Arm.

Canadian bacon

1) A cut of pork loin leaner than the fatty bacon normally served throughout Canada and the U.S. 2) *Peameal bacon,* so-called by Americans and confused Canadians. 3) A 1995 comedy film directed by Michael Moore in which a fictional U.S. president declares war on Canada to distract the electorate from domestic problems and plummeting approval ratings. As a point of information, whether you order bacon and eggs in Canada or the U.S., you'll get the same kind of bacon.

Canadian Club

A potent and popular brand of whiskey distilled and aged near Windsor, Ontario.

Canadian Tire (a.k.a. "Crappy Tire")

A publically traded Canadian company founded in 1925 that retails in home wares, sporting goods, automotive equipment, tools, hardware, camping supplies and pretty much anything else you can think of except food. It has been estimated that 85 percent of Canadians live within a 15-minute drive of one of the 465 stores nationwide.

"You know, Bob, there's a lot more to *Canadian Tire* than just tires."

"That's right, Alice. You can give like Santa and save like Scrooge."
"It's for days like today."
"It's the store for people like us."
"Irritating Slogans: Aisle Six."

Canadian Tire money

Canadian Tire's customer loyalty program—in which five percent of the pre-tax purchase total is given to the customer in paper bills that can then be redeemed at face value for in-store merchandise. Available in whopping denominations of 5 cents, 10 cents, 25 cents, 50 cents and $1 or $2, *Canadian Tire money* is printed on paper that feels frustratingly like real money to hopeful hands searching through otherwise empty pockets. Also, since its introduction in 1958, children too young to know better have come across their parents' stash and think they've hit the jackpot.

"Good day to you shopkeeper. My friend and I have come to your fine *dépanneur* to purchase this bag of *ketchup-flavoured chips*, this *Jos. Louis* and these *Smartie*s. I trust we have enough currency to complete this transaction?"

"*Sorry,* son, but that's Canadian Tire money."

"*Merde!*"

CanCon

Short for "Canadian Content." In 1971, Canada's broadcast regulating body, the Canadian Radio-Television and Telecommunications Commission (mercifully shortened to CRTC), introduced requirements for Canadian TV and radio stations to broadcast a certain amount of material created by Canadians. Guided by the *MAPL* rule, radio stations could determine whether a given song met its *CanCon* quota. Similar rules applied to TV. The *McKenzie Brothers* themselves are the result of *CanCon* requirements.

"What's the topic for today's show, Bob?"

"Well, Doug, today's show is about *CanCon, eh?*"

"Let's sing a song about *toques* and *beer* and *back bacon.*"

"Okay, but, like, the music and lyrics have to be written and performed by a Canadian artist and produced in Canada, *eh?*"

CANDU

A kind of nuclear reactor designed and built in Canada, but sold extensively abroad as well as at home. Its name is short for Canada Deuterium Uranium, though many people equate it with some kind of pun on "Can-do."

canola

1) A modified member of the rapeseed family.
2) Oil derived from this plant and used for cooking and food-processing as well as being used to make rubber, fuel and lubricants. The name was coined in the late 1970s and is short for Canadian Oil, Low Acid.

Canuck

1) Slang for "Canadian," as either a noun ("Are you a *Canuck?*") or an adjective ("*Canuck* girls kick ass!"). It can be used derisively as well, with some anti-Canadian American commentators referring to "Soviet *Canuck*istan." On the other hand, Canadians are their own best rehabilitators as is shown by the creation of the superhero character Captain *Canuck*.

Cape Breton pork pie

A date-filled dessert contained by short pastry.
"Care for some *Cape Breton pork pie?*"
"Has it got pork in it?"
"Nope, dates actually."
"Is it a pie?"
"More of a tart really."
"Is it from Cape Breton?"
"Maybe."
"Sure, I'll have some."

Car!

Heard for untold generations during *street hockey* games all across Canada to warn of approaching automobiles. Upon its utterance, the net is pulled off to one side and the players stand at the curb. Only when the car has passed and the net replaced is heard the cry *Game on!*

Cariboo

Not to be confused with *caribou*, this spelling with the double "o" refers to a large area of south-central

BC originally extending from the juncture of the Quesnel and Fraser rivers to the Cariboo mountains. Nowadays though, it refers to an even larger area stretching from Lillooet to Prince George.

caribou

1) An antlered deer native to North America's tundra regions. 2) In Québec, an alcoholic drink made from one part red wine and six parts grain alcohol.

"What's wrong with that *caribou?*"

"I think she got into the *caribou.*"

Carnaval (de Québec)

The world's largest winter carnival, held in Québec City since 1894, Le Carnaval runs for 17 days starting on either the last Friday in January or the first Friday in February. It is a beloved tradition for Québecers, and for *anglo* school children in the rest of Canada, it is one of the first Québec traditions they learn about when starting to take French lessons. The *Carnaval*'s snowman mascot, *Monsieur Bonhomme*, is easily recognized by most Canadians.

Casey and Finnegan

Two hand puppets who inhabit a tree house behind *Mr. Dressup's* house. Casey was a child made from paper maché (generally assumed to be a boy) while Finnegan was a sock-puppet style dog with floppy ears. The phrase *Casey and*

Finnegan is instantly recognizable by at least two generations of TV-watching Canadian children since grown to adulthood, many of them still obsessed with getting to see what the inside of the tree house looked like.

casse-croute

French Canadian (or, as some say, Canadian French) for "snack bar." Depending on the particular part of Québec you're in, you may have better luck making yourself understood by simply saying, "snek barrr" with an exaggerated Québecois accent (seriously).

catawumpus

In PEI, an adjective meaning askew or out of order. Overheard on a windy day:
"Your *cow's breakfast* is all *catawumpus*."
"I beg your pardon?"
"Not from around here are ya?"

CBC

Short for "Canadian Broadcasting Corporation," a.k.a. "The Mother Corps," "The Corps," "The Corpse," and allegedly once referred to on-air as the "Canadian Broadcorping Castration" but probably not really. The *CBC* is Canada's public broadcaster, inspiring fierce loyalty, indifference bordering on contempt and downright hostility—sometimes all at once and in the same person. The persistent reader will find many other references to the *CBC* herein.

CEGEP

In Québec, short for, "collège d'enseignement général et professionnel." *CEGEP* is an institution that offers two-year programs in university preparation but is most well known for its three-year trade and technical programs.

cent a pound or on the ground

A slogan coined by BC fruit growers in 1933 during their first collective negotiations with packing houses that frequently paid less than a *cent a pound* for apples.

Centennial

Confederation took place on July 1, 1867. A hundred years later, Canadians proudly and happily kicked off a year-long celebration of their country. With events and projects sponsored by all three levels of government, as well as a genuine sense of excitement from regular Canadians, the *Centennial* left its mark on our communities, parks, hearts and minds. It is often cited as one of the final years that Canadians experienced a sense of optimism before the onset of the 1970s. Pierre Berton famously called it "the last good year."

Centennial coins

A special 1967 minting of Canadian coins struck in celebration of the *Centennial* and showing various animals of Canada. At the time of writing (more than 40 years later), one still receives the occasional *Centennial* coin in pocket change, especially the penny with its majestic...pigeon in mid-flight (don't be fooled by those who call it a rock dove—this is just an elitist way of saying "pigeon"). The other animals were a rabbit, on the nickel; a mackerel, on the dime; a lynx, on the quarter; a wolf, on the 50-cent piece; and a Canada goose, on the silver dollar.

Centennial project

Centennial projects were generally funded by one or more levels of government and covered the entire spectrum of Canadian culture, including literature, music, film, television, performance arts and even the construction of buildings and parks. If you're walking through a Canadian city and see an odd sculpture that might have looked futuristic in 1967, it's probably a *Centennial project.*

centre (vs. center)

Centre is the Canadian, and therefore correct, way of spelling this word as opposed to the American "center."

centre ice (in Québec, "centre hice")

A hockey term denoting the centre of the rink where the puck is dropped at the beginning of each period or after each goal. American readers should note that it is spelled "cent**re** ice" and not "cent**er** ice."

century house

A home that is approximately 100 years old. They

are something of a rarity in Canada because of our collective tendency to tear down our past.

Century Sam

A cartoon prospector character created for British Columbia's centennial in 1958.
"Is that a laughing *Mennonite* on your button?"
"That's *Century Sam!*"

CFL

Canadian Football League.

chalet

In Québec, a holiday cottage. "C'est le *chalet* de ma tante." (It is my aunt's cottage.)

(la) Chasse-galerie

The French Canadian name for the Legend of the Flying Canoe, which tells the story of a band of *voyageurs* who want to see their sweethearts on New Year's Eve. They make a pact with the devil, who gives them the power to paddle their canoe through the air at fantastic speeds in order to travel the 300 miles and be back in time for work the next day. In exchange, the *voyageurs* promise that during the journey they will not take the Lord's name in vain, nor allow their canoe to touch any church steeples. In most versions of the story, the outward leg of the journey goes well, but once they have landed and rung in the New Year, one of them starts to drunkenly swear on the return voyage. In some tellings of the tale, they toss the offending paddler overboard and continue on to get home safely, but in others they are doomed to paddle the skies forever. The original version of the tale involved a nobleman named Gallery who loved to hunt so much that he would not attend Sunday mass and so was forever doomed to run through the skies, chased by hellish beasts. *La Chasse-galerie* translates literally as "The Hunt of Gallery," and it is from this original story that the legend derives its name. *La Chasse-galerie* is referenced on the label for "Maudite" beer, showing the damned (literally) *voyageurs* frantically paddling either away from or towards eternal damnation. (See also *Maudit!*)

cheechako

Chinook jargon. 1) A noun meaning "newcomer" or "outsider," having a mildly contemptuous connotation. "Who are all these *cheechakos* arriving with the their *hyas cultus chic chics?*" 2) An adjective to describe something relating to a newcomer or outsider. "This *cheechako chikamin* is *cultus.*"

Cheezies

1) A brand name for puffed cheese snacks that are toxic orange in colour but highly delicious in taste. 2) The same way that the brand name Kleenex has come to be used for any tissue product, *Cheezies* is now used to describe any number of other "cheese curl" snacks. Overheard in Canadian variety store:

"And I'll use some o' this *funny money* to buy these Cheetos."

"We call them *Cheezies* here, Tex."

cheque

A promissory note for money written against the issuer's bank account. Americans spell it "check" and, as well as the meaning above, confusingly also use "check" instead of the more sensible *bill* when asking to pay up in restaurants.

"Can you check to see what happened to my check?"

"I can, but that's not a *cheque* is it? We don't accept payment by *cheque.*"

"I thought that in Canada I could pay the check by check."

"You'd better check more carefully next time, Bill."

chesterfield

Couch. Although slowly falling out of use, this was once a sure way of identifying a Canadian. While people in other countries use *chesterfield* to describe a sofa or couch whose arms are at the same height as the back, Canadians say *chesterfield* to describe any domestic seating appurtenance that fits more than two.

"Where can I put my luggage?"

"Over by the *chesterfield.*"

"Who's Chester, where is his field, and why should I put my luggage there?"

chic chic

Chinook jargon for "wheel" or "wagon," so-called from the creaking sound of the wheels. Overheard near the turn of the last century:

"These *cheechako chic chics* don't go *chic chic,* they go put-put."

chiclets

Hockey slang for "teeth," so termed because they resemble the little white squares of chewing gum whose brand name was Chiclets.

"*Sorry* I knocked your *chiclets* out when I deliberately smashed you across the face with my stick."

"It's all part of the game, man. I wish they'd just let us play instead of having all these rules."

chicot

A dead tree or dead part of a tree (from the French for "stump").

"That *cheechako lumberjack* François seems kind of...useless."

"We call him *chicot*."

chikamin

Chinook jargon for "metal" or "money."

"How much *chikamin* do you want for your *skookum chic chic?*"

chimo

An Inuit greeting word meaning variously 1) "Hello." 2) "Are you friendly?" (when spoken with one open-palmed hand circling your heart). 3) A greeting or toast still used occasionally by some Canadians. 4) The cheer of the Canadian Military Engineers.

Chinook

1) A kind of salmon native to BC. 2) A warm, dry wind during winter months, especially on the Prairies. People generally look forward to the rise in temperature that a *Chinook* brings.

"Would you stop breathing down the back of my neck?"

"I'm not—it's a *Chinook*."

"Oh well, that's different then."

Chinook jargon

An informal trading language that emerged in 19th century BC. With Salish and Nootka Aboriginal traders interacting with French and English traders, some sort of common language had to be found, and *Chinook jargon* was it. At its peak around 1900, approximately 100,000 people were using it, but 20 years later it was all but gone. The *Chinook* word still in use most frequently today is *skookum*, but you will find many other examples in this book.

chocolate bar

What Americans call a "candy bar," Canadians call a *chocolate bar*.

"I'd like to buy this candy bar."

"Sure. But just so you know, we call them *chocolate*

bars up here."

"I see. Thanks. Now what colour money do I pay you with for that?"

"One of those reddish ones with the guy with the moustache should do it."

chowderhead

An insulting term originating in early logging camps to describe loggers who had previously been sailors.

"Why is it that whenever we fell a tree, that guy calls 'Land ho' instead of 'Timber'?"

"Because he's a *chowderhead*, that's why."

chuck

1) *Chinook jargon* for "freshwater." 2) Used nowadays by British Columbians to refer to the ocean, sometimes also called *salt chuck*.

"Don't fall in the *chuck, chowderhead*."

chunk out

1) A former logging term meaning "to clear away debris," especially fallen trees. "*Chunk out* this section of road so we can haul the logs through." 2) Getting into a fight. "I *chunked out* the room."

CIL spinner

In BC, a fishing lure of the explosive variety, being a stick of dynamite detonated under water to kill fish, so-called for an explosives plant owned by Canadian Industries Limited.

"My favourite fishing lure is the *CIL spinner*.

The fish like it so much they just gently **float** to the surface."

cipaille

Pronounced "sea pie," this marks one of those rare instances in which French has borrowed a phrase from English—"sea pie"—and bastardized the spelling. It is a thick savoury pie with alternating layers of meat and pastry. It is not clear whether the recipe ever called for seafood.

"Does the *cipaille* have seafood in it?"
"Nope, just some *bush salmon*."

City of the Newly Wed and Nearly Dead

A frighteningly accurate description of Victoria, BC. Not surprisingly, people who live in that city don't actually refer to it in these terms, and really, who can blame them (even if it is true)?

"And where are you going on your honey-moon?"
"City of the Newly Wed and Nearly Dead."
"Have fun at the *flower count*."

civic holiday

A holiday that is commonly observed but not leg-islated. In Canada, the first Monday in August is generally taken as a *civic holiday* (except in Qué-bec and PEI). Overheard in the latter:

"Allo monsieur. I 'ave been driving all day on the *autoroute* hall the way from Québec and nowhere can I find a roadside stand selling *pomme de terres*. Not until I 'ave reached here 'ave I seen

the roadside stands selling *pommes de terre*. Pour-
quoi that is?"

"It's a *civic holiday* today, that's why. The rest of
the country gets a holiday, but not you and
I, oh no."

civil

Descriptive of calm, pleasant or favourable weather
conditions, especially on the coast or at sea.

"It's very *civil* today."

"Yup. Not *mauzy*."

"Nope."

"Nor *snotty*."

"Nope."

"Not a *drash* of rain in on the horiz—"

"No, there isn't. And in fact, **all** of those are reasons I said it was *civil* today!"

Clamato juice

A brand name of clam broth and tomato juice
crucial to a *Bloody Caesar*. While *Clamato juice* was
invented in the U.S., with the Caesar's invention
in Calgary, Canada created a voracious demand
for it. It is included here because if you are travelling in the U.S. and ask for *Clamato juice*, someone
may look at you strangely and quite rightly ask
why anyone should want to mix clam squeezings
and tomato innards.

clap-dish

In Newfoundland, an old gossip.

"So then, I heard it from my sister's husband's

cousin's priest's daughter's dog-walker's cleaning lady and—"

"Shut it, you old *clap-dish*."

clever

In Newfoundland, handsome or impressive. Complimentary Newfoundlanders might say to someone immaculately attired and groomed, "My, but don't you look *clever* today."

clobber

In Newfoundland, the untidy, messy remains as of a meal.

"Let's clean up the *clobber*."

clucker

In PEI, 1) A fussy hen thought to be looking for eggs to sit on. 2) A fussy person thought to be looking for some insignificant lost item.

"Losing that little plastic thing off the end of your shoelace is nothing to get upset about. Now stop looking for it you silly *clucker*."

"It's called a ferrule—it has a name, and if it has a name, it's important enough to look for."

clumper/clumpet

In maritime Canada, 1) a small iceberg floating in the bay. 2) A large sheet (or "pan") of ice floating in the bay.

"All those *clumpers* are perfect for a nice game of *steppycock*."

"I'm from Ontario. What are you talking about?"

Coast to coast (in hockey)

1) When a player skates from his own end to that of the opposing team without ever passing the puck. "Looks like he's taking it *coast to coast*, Don." 2) Descriptive of an action-packed hockey game in which the puck sees lots of action in both ends of the rink. "It's *coast to coast*, tonight, Ron." (See also *end to end*.)

cod

A North Atlantic saltwater *fish* of the genus *Gadus morhua* and the mainstay of Canada's east-coast commercial fishing industry since its inception. In Newfoundland, it is generally referred to simply as *fish*. It has also worked its way into various expressions (see entries below).

Codland

Newfoundland, to westerners of yore. This expression seems to have been in use at various spots in the Prairies in and around 1900. Overheard at that time:

"Cattle breeding is just so expensive."

"You could always try *fish* ranching in *Codland*."

codswallop

Nonsense. It seems to be a favourite of Canadian politicians.

"Mr. Speaker, that is the biggest load of *codswallop* I've ever heard." (See also *blatherskite* and *fuddle duddle*.)

C

Coffee Crisp

The brand name of a chocolate bar consisting of coffee-flavoured cream and layered wafers and coated in chocolate. First marketed here in 1938, *Coffee Crisp* was only available in Canada until 2006, but since then has begun to be distributed abroad. Past advertising slogans have entered the Canadian consciousness:

"*Coffee Crisp* makes a nice, light snack."

Or "How do you like your coffee?—Crisp."

coffee row

In Saskatchewan, a regular gathering of people to drink coffee and exchange gossip, especially in rural areas.

"So, I heard from Marge's nephew's girlfriend's skating instructor's accountant that Marge has eloped to *The Peg*."

"How do you know all this?"

"*Coffee row.*"

coho

A species of salmon important to the BC fishing industry.

"Have a good day fishin'?"

"Caught me a nice *coho*."

colcannon night

Hallowe'en to some in Newfoundland, so-called because a dish of mixed vegetables (usually including cabbage) called "colcannon" is traditionally eaten on this night.

"Look far and wide on *colcannon night*,
For ghosts and ghouls to set you affright."

Come back again when you can't stay so long

An insult attributed to an angry resident of Lunenberg, Nova Scotia, meaning rather obviously, "Good riddance and don't let the door hit you on the way out."

come from away (CFA)

A Maritimism meaning more-or-less "not from around here."
"I can't believe your brother-in-law doesn't know what *steppycock* is."
"Did you try calling it *copy?*"
"Didn't know that either."
"How about *boggers?*"
"That neither."
"Well, you have to cut him some slack. He's *come from away* and ain't so smart."

come-along

A portable, hand-operated winch that can be attached to a stable object like a tree or fencepost in order to move a heavy load for a short distance.
"Hitch up that *come-along* to *chunk out* this load of *pecker poles*."

concession

A term used primarily in Ontario and Québec to denote a parcel of surveyed land subdivided yet again into lots.

C

concession line

A property line separating two *concessions* and often marked by painted iron stakes pounded into the ground, a post and wire fence or, more pleasantly, a line of deliberately planted or blazed trees. Those familiar with this term sometimes need to be reminded that not everyone knows what it means.

"Your property doesn't start until the next *concession line*."

"Look, I've just moved here *from away*, and I'd like it if you'd stop trynna make a *confloption* out of all this and talk like a *Canuck*."

concession road

A road cut around one or more sides of a *concession*, usually directly on a *concession line* that has been specially designated so that neither of the two property owners on either side will suffer a reduction in acreage.

confloption

In Newfoundland, a state of confusion.

"My uncle went to Ontario and bought some land and said everything there was one big *confloption*. They actually separate property with *confloption* lines."

"That can't be true." It isn't; see *concession line* above.)

construction day

In Québec, a holiday taken by construction workers

during the last two weeks of July and observed by many other professions as well.

"So you work in demolition, but you get *construction day* off just like the rest of us?"

Co-op

1) In high schools, short for Co-operative Education Program, in which students receive academic credits for work placements in an industry related to their studies. Most students love Co-op because it gets them out of the classroom and off school grounds altogether.

"I thought you had a *spare* this *aft.*"

"Got *Co-op.*"

"Same thing."

2) In the Prairies, a central, grocery-vending depot run co-operatively.

"I have to go to the *Co-op* for bread."

co-ordinates

Informal slang for contact information expressed alphanumerically, such as phone numbers, mailing and e-mail addresses.

"Send me your *co-ordinates* and we'll get in touch."

"My *co-ordinate*s? I'm standing right here in front of you."

copy

In the Maritimes, a game played by leaping from iceberg to iceberg, copying the moves of another person. Think of "Follow the Leader," but with a much greater risk of hypothermia. "Now, to celebrate Billy not drownin' the last time we played, how about a nice game of *copy?* Bob, you've just gotten the cast off your leg—you lead."

Cossacks of Upper Canada

A flippant nickname for...*lumberjacks*, character-ized by the writer E.C. Guillet as "an incorrigible...race of mortals...whom, however, I would name the *Cossacks of Upper Canada*."

cottage country

In central Canada, an area in which there are many cottages, usually in close proximity to one of the Great Lakes or other inland bodies of water.

coureur de bois

French for "runner of the woods." A fur trader, especially one employed by the Hudson's Bay Company during the late 17th and early 18th centuries. Along with a passing knowledge of the *seigneurial system*, knowing what *coureur de bois* means is often the sum total of their history retained by Canadians older than 25.

cow grease

Butter in the western Canada of yesteryear. This term was probably an endless source of confusion and revulsion for people new to the Prairies.
"Care for some *cow grease* on your bread?"
"Er...thank you, but I should prefer to have butter instead."

cow juice

In western Canada of yesteryear, milk.

"Care for a nice glass of *cow juice?*"

"Oh...uh...well, that's very nice of you, but I wouldn't want to rob your crops of the fertilizer they so richly deserve."

Cowichan cashmere

In a BC logging community called Cowichan Lake, some sarcastic logger started calling his grey cotton undershirt *Cowichan cashmere,* and the name stuck, eventually coming into use by *Wet-coast* dry wits.

"This *Cowichan cashmere* feels so soft against my skin."

"Dude, it's an undershirt that you've washed so often I can see through it!"

Cowichan sweater

A heavy sweater of grey, homespun, undyed wool often embroidered with figures of animal, birds, whales and plants. Made by the Coast Salish of Vancouver Island's Cowichan Valley, they are a popular gift for tourists visiting the area, though sometimes a source of semantic bafflement.

"I think I'd like to buy one of those *Cowichan sweaters.*"

"Gesundheit."

cow's breakfast

A wide-brimmed straw hat worn to keep the sun off and usually referred to as such in rural areas.

139

Overheard as a city slicker visits her country cousin:

"Oops, my *cow's breakfast* fell off."

"Hadn't you better call the veterinarian?"

Cowtown

Calgary, probably so-called because of its proximity to the cattle ranchers of the Prairies and, no doubt, the annual Calgary Stampede.

coyote

Although Canadians and Americans spell this the same way and it means the same thing, one key difference is pronunciation. You may hear both on either side of the border, but Canadians are more likely to say "KY-oht," while Americans are more likely to say "ky-OH-tee."

"Watch out for that 'ky-oht,' my *Yankee* friend."

"You mean that 'ky-oh-tee,' my *Canuck* buddy?"

"I mean that specimen of *Canis latrans* that has now bitten you on the ankle."

CPP

Canada Pension Plan. Just what it says, although in a few years, it won't be.

CPR

Canadian Pacific Railway. Completed in 1885, the CPR is an integral part of Canada's history, since it provided an efficient way for people to travel and ship goods from one coast to the other. Gordon Lightfoot immortalized it in song with his

"Canadian Railroad Trilogy," and Pierre Berton recounted its construction in two books: *The National Dream* and *The Last Spike*.

CPR strawberries

Stewed prunes, formerly served as breakfast fruit on company trains and steamboats, also often used in logging and construction camps because they kept well. One can only imagine the hilarity that must have ensued when over-tired porters offered them to travellers on posh passenger trains.

"Would you care for some *CPR strawberries* ma'am?"

"They sound delicious. However did you get them at this time of year?"

"Boiling, ma'am."

cretons

A tasty, spiced pork spread, often eaten on toast in Québec, especially at breakfast. For first-time breakfast eaters in *la belle province*, *cretons* goes from being a puzzling menu item to a delicious surprise.

crop checking

Especially in BC, an all-purpose excuse for a drive in the country.

"What are you doing for your date tomorrow, dear?"

"We're going *crop checking*."

"Well, that's a very industrious thing for two

young people to do, and on a Saturday night too!"

crowbar palace

A jailhouse, especially in the North of long ago. "Klondike Bill jumped my claim and earned himself a stay in the *crowbar palace*."

Crown

1) The federal government. 2) Any of the provincial governments. "The *Crown* is pursuing legal proceedings in the matter."

Crown corporation

A corporation owned by the federal or provincial governments. The *CBC* and Canada Post are *Crown corporations*.

Crown land

Land owned by the federal or provincial governments, sometimes with the specific purpose of protecting wilderness spots from development by humans.

CSIS (pron: SEE-sis)

Canadian Security Intelligence Service. Founded in 1984, *CSIS* is Canada's spy agency, whose responsibilities include, among other things, counter-intelligence and counter-terrorism. With a reputation for making very public mistakes, *CSIS* is not as covert as many Canadians might hope. In the most famous incident, sensitive documents were stolen from the car of an employee attending a Toronto *Maple Leafs* game (*Go Leafs, Go!*). The fact that many former agents and even informants are listed on Wikipedia should serve as a stark reminder that neither "S" in *CSIS* stands for "secret."

cube van

A truck used for moving cargo, having a cab for the driver and passengers, but with a separate rectangular box-shaped container for the cargo. In the U.S. they are called "box trucks." Overheard at a Canadian truck rental firm:
"I'd like to rent me a box truck, please."
"Certainly, sir. We have several fine *cube vans* that you can pack all your boxes into."

cultus

Chinook jargon for worthless, bad, defective, stinking, dirty, and so forth.
"This *salt chuck* is *cultus* for drinking."

cultus cooley

Chinook jargon for a pleasure stroll with no purpose or destination.
"Shall we do a bit of *crop checking* this afternoon?"
"Yes, and then perhaps a nice *cultus cooley*."

cultus potlatch

A gift for which nothing is expected in return, generally of little actual value, but sincerely meant.

"Wow, thanks for this wad of *Canadian Tire money*."
"Just a little *cultus potlatch*. It was cluttering up
our kitchen drawer anyway."

cutlery

Forks, knives and spoons. While Canadians also
say "silverware" and "flatware," Americans use
these last two terms almost exclusively, and so
cutlery might be a bit of a puzzler.

da da da DAH da DAH

A phonetic rendition of the beginning of the musical theme from *Hockey Night in Canada* (the actual title is "The Hockey Theme"). It is instantly recognizable to millions of Canadians, from the *CBC*'s flagship hockey broadcast, and has been called "Canada's second national anthem." Premiered in 1968, its rights were sold to CTV in 2008, and it is now heard before hockey games on CTV cable affiliate TSN.

date squares

A dessert with a foundation of oatmeal, surmounted by date filling and capped with crumble topping. It is known as *matrimonial cake* in the Prairies.

defood

To vomit. "You'll have to excuse my husband not being here to greet you. He's in the washroom *defooding*."

Degrassi

A popular TV franchise, comparable to *Beachcombers*

in both its longevity and its capacity to annoy people who don't give a crap about it. The main series are *The Kids of Degrassi Street*, *Degrassi Junior High*, *Degrassi High* and *Degrassi: The Next Generation*. Influential overseas and ever-popular here at home, the *Degrassi* series has influenced two separate generations of Canadians.

deke

1) In hockey, a misleading move in which a puck carrier fools the goaltender into letting in a goal. Usually this is accomplished by zigging, zagging, winding up for a fake shot or just being a generally wily player. "He totally *deked* him out and scored." 2) Also in hockey, to unexpectedly elude another player by skating around him. "He *deked* around him."

dépanneur (pron: day-pan-URR) (dep)

In Québec, a variety store selling milk, cigarettes and beer. In France, a *dépanneur* is a mechanic who fixes cars; from "dépanner" (to break down). How it came to mean "variety store" in Québec remains something of a mystery. It is used by both *anglos* and *francophones*, occasionally even outside of *la belle province*. "I'm goin' down to the *dep* for smokes. Need anything?"

Department

A branch of the federal government with responsibility for a particular portfolio (such as *Department* of Defense, *Department* of Finance, and so on). Many Canadians have trouble remembering that *Departments* are federal and *Ministries* are provincial.

Department of Holidays

A sometime colloquialism for the Ministry of Transportation in BC, due to the high number of government employees apparently standing idly by the side of the road.

Diefenbunkers

A series of seven bomb shelters built during the Cold War at the behest of then Prime Minister John Diefenbaker, presumably to allow the smooth governance of what little of Canada would remain after a supposed nuclear attack. The only extant *Diefenbunker*, in Carp, Ontario, has been converted into a museum.

digby chicken

A Nova Scotia term for smoked, salted herring eaten as snacks and named after the town of Digby, Nova Scotia. This is yet another Maritimism guaranteed to confuse those *come from away*.
"Have you got some sort of nice seafood snack?"
"How about some *digby chickens*."
"I said **seafood** and **snack**, not **poultry** and **meal-for-two**!"

digestive cookie/biscuit

A round, whole wheat, semi-sweet cookie popular in Canada, the UK and other Commonwealth countries, but unknown in the U.S. except to devout Anglophiles. They are called digestive cookies because, when they were invented in 1799, the ingredient, bicarbonate of soda, was thought to aid in digestion.

dilsey

In PEI of yore, a good-looking young woman.

"That Susan's a proper *dilsey.*"

"Yup. Really knows how to dig a potato, too."

dipsy doodle

In hockey, the same as a *deke*, but engendering much fancier footwork, greater stick-handling legerdemain and veritable prestidigitation of the puck.

Distant Early Warning/DEW (pron: DOO) Line

A series of radar stations across Canada's northern reaches. Intended to warn of approaching Cold War Soviet bombers, the *DEW Line* was made redundant by the advent of Intercontinental Ballistic Missiles. Overheard in Carp, Ontario, during the 1960s:

"If there's a warning from the *DEW Line*, I'm headin' for the *Diefenbunker.*"

doesn't have all his cornflakes in the same box

Said of someone who is, perhaps, just a little off centre; who may not have all of their wits about them. Overheard on Parliament Hill in the 1940s:

"Have you heard that the prime minister talks to the ghosts of his mother **and** his dog? *Doesn't have all his cornflakes in the same box.*"

donkeyman

In old-time logging lingo, the logger who ran a "donkey engine," so-called because it did the work that until recently was done by donkeys and other beasts of burden. The donkey engine hauled logs from one part of a logging site to another. Since large distances were involved, the *donkeyman* was usually too far away to see the *hooktender* (the person who bundled the logs together for hauling) and so relied on a relay system whereby the *hooktender* signalled the *whistle punk*, who then blew a whistle to let the *donkeyman* know the engine could be turned on to haul away.

don't bust a gusset

Don't lose your temper/Don't work too hard. A gusset was a small V-shaped cloth insert at the back of men's trousers in the 19th and early 20th centuries. If the person wearing the pants gained or lost weight, the gusset could be let out or taken in.

Don't change. I wanna forget you as you are

An insult, seeming to require no further explanation. *"Be sure to come back when you can't stay so long."*

"Oh yeah? Well, *don't change. I wanna forget you as you are.*"

don't let your antifreeze

A nonsense farewell in PEI, seemingly a punning take on "Don't let your auntie freeze."

Don't like the weather? Just wait five minutes

In Vancouver and Calgary, a rhetorical phrase reflecting the city's fickle weather patterns, being capable of rain, snow and sunshine all within a few minutes of one another.

dooryard

An expression in Carleton County, New Brunswick, to delineate an outdoor area of the home not in use for farming, presumably a yard located just outside the back door. "You and your friends take your *two-four* out in the *dooryard* to drink it."

double-double

When ordering coffee, to ask for two creams and two sugars. "One small black coffee, two medium regular and one large *double-double.*" In recent years this has become a famous Canadianism and has even been added to *The Canadian Oxford Dictionary.* There are unconfirmed reports that U.S. soldiers serving in Afghanistan overheard their Canadian comrades requesting coffee this way (in Afghanistan's only *Tim Hortons*) and thought they were speaking some sort of code. The

Americans reportedly then invented their own slang "quadruple quadruple," which is presumably equivalent to *four by four* (see also *triple-triple*).

doughnut vs. donut

The truth is that you'll see both spellings on either side of the border, but Canadians lean somewhat towards "doughnut" when spelling out the name of this favourite snack, whereas Americans are more likely to spell it "donut."

drain the main vein

To pee (generally used by men). "Whew! We're halfway through that *two-four*. Time to *drain the main vein.*"

drash of rain

In PEI, 1) (noun) a heavy shower of rain. "We got soaked by a *drash* of rain." 2) (verb) of the sea or rough lake water, to splash violently and soakingly. "The waves *drashed* all over them."

dream in Technicolor

To be wildly unrealistic.

"Have you heard Jen's latest plans? After she becomes a private detective, she's gonna manage a Latin jazz troupe and then open an arctic orchid sanctuary."

"She's *dreamin' in Technicolor.*" (Note: Sticklers for Canadian spelling should note that, since it is a trademarked name, "Technicolor" cannot be spelled "Technicolour.")

drive shed

In Ontario, a large shed used to store vehicles, tools and other sundry necessities of Canadian life. "Calm down. I'm sure I've got an ice-saw and some bagpipes somewhere out in the *drive shed.*"

drunk as a thousand dollars

In old-time BC logging communities, very drunk indeed. When loggers rolled into town on payday, some of them spent most of their wages getting drunk, and so this expression indicates both the cost and degree of drunkenness being described. "SawTooth Pete's asleep in the gutter again. He's *drunk as a thousand dollars.*"

dumb as two short planks

Descriptive of extreme stupidity. A certain type of person, upon cutting a piece of wood too short for its intended purpose, will immediately take a second piece of wood and do the same thing in the belief that making the same mistake twice will somehow solve the problem.

"The first time he caught his head in the door, he figured it was just cause the door happened to be in an inconvenient spot right then."

"Dumb as two short planks."

Duo-Tang

A brand of folder for holding three-ring binder paper with two little metal prongs positioned to poke through one of three holes and bend in opposite directions to hold the paper in. For school-going Canadians of a certain age, oft-heard words were, "Put these handouts into your *Duo-Tang*."

Dutchie

A square *doughnut* with raisins in it, having a dandruff-like flakey white frosting and being generally very dense, especially in its day-old form.

"What kind of *doughnut* do you want—maybe a *Dutchie?*"

"No."

East Coast

A general term for Canada's Atlantic provinces and environs.

eat what you can, and can what you can't

In BC, a slogan exhorting those who could to conserve food during the Depression and subsequently, World War II.

Eaton's doesn't tell Simpson's their business

In PEI, 1) I'm not going to tell you what I'm doing.

"How come your potatoes are better than my potatoes?"

"Eaton's doesn't tell Simpsons their business."

2) A maxim cautioning blabbermouths to hold their tongues.

"Should we tell them why we think our potatoes are better than their potatoes?"

"Eaton's doesn't tell Simpsons their business."

Eaton's and Simpson's, now defunct, were two Canadian department stores of great repute. This saying almost certainly derives from the American

"Macey's doesn't tell Gimbels their business," also in reference to competing retailers.

eats sawdust and shits two-by-fours

Descriptive of someone who is very, very (very) tough.

"That's the kid who plays *steppycock* in his bare feet."

"When he grows up he'll *eat sawdust and shit two-by-fours*."

eavestrough

A metal trough running along the edge of a building's roof, meant to collect and drain rainwater. Americans call them "rain gutters," but in Canada "gutter" is reserved for that space between the curb and the street where we're all told we'll wind up if we don't eat our vegetables, get a job, stop swearing, and so forth.

Edmonchuk

Edmonton, Alberta. "Chuk" is a common suffix in Ukrainian surnames, and Edmonton has more than its fair share of Ukrainian Canadians.

"Well, I'm off to *Edmonchuk* for the weekend."

"Have a perogie for me."

eh

An informal interjection, famous around the world and in Canada as something that Canadians frequently say. Although usually followed by a question mark when written, its utterance is rarely intended to pose an actual question. For a fuller exploration of this word, see Chapter Four, "How's It Goin', *Eh?*" Briefly, *eh* can be used in any of the following situations. 1) Statements of opinion: "Nice day, *eh?*" 2) Statements of fact: "It goes over here, *eh?*" 3) Commands: "Open the window, *eh?*" 4) Exclamations: "What a game, *eh?*" 5) Questions: "What are they trying to do, *eh?*" 6) To mean "pardon": "*Eh?* What did you say?" 7) In fixed expressions: "I know, *eh?*"; "Thanks, *eh?*" 8) Insults: "You're a real snob, *eh?*" 9) Accusations: "You took the last piece, *eh?*" 10) Storytelling (also called the "narrative *eh*"): "This guy is up on the 27th floor, *eh*, then he gets out on the ledge, *eh…*"

elastic (band)

A rubber band, also simply referred to as "an *elastic.*" Overheard between two cross-border friends:

"Hand me an *elastic* would you?"

"An *elastic* what?"

"An *elastic band*, brainiac!"

"Oh, a rubber band. You see, in America, we generally use *elastic* only as an adjective, and here in Canada you use it as a noun as well. What do you need it for?"

"So I can flick it at you."

elevener

In Newfoundland, a snack or alcoholic drink consumed at eleven in the morning. While posh drinkers of gin and sherry may have their "elevenses," working folks on *The Rock* and briny mariners at sea have their *elevener*. "Time for the *elevener*. Care for a cup of *callibogus?*"

Employment Insurance (or EI)

Formerly known as *Unemployment Insurance*, *UI* and *UIC* (Unemployment Insurance Commission), *Employment Insurance* is a federal program whereby employers deduct contributions (along with income tax and *CPP*) from an employee's paycheque with the intent that, if the worker becomes unemployed, he or she can then redeem these funds by applying to the appropriate federal department. In reality, of course, it is never this easy.

empty barrels make the most noise

While being literally true, this expression refers figuratively to people who talk the talk but haven't taken a single step towards actually walking the walk.

"Lemme tell ya, me and the boys we're gonna do all this research into acoustics and all that and we're gonna build our own echo chamber in my garage out of pipe cleaners and Popsicle sticks 'cause we're all geniuses and y'know what we expect to find out?"

"Empty barrels make the most noise?"

"That's right."

E

end to end

In hockey, 1) When a player skates from his own end to that of the opposing team without ever passing the puck. "He's going *end to end*, Don." 2) Descriptive of an action-packed hockey game in which the puck sees lots of action in both ends of the rink. "It's *end to end*, tonight, Ron." (See also *coast to coast*.)

equal

In Newfoundland, part of a colloquial expression meaning, "It's all the same to me."
"Do you want us to sterilize your wound with *moose milk* or *screech*?"
"It's all *equal* to me."

Everything's jake

Everything's good. It's difficult to imagine anyone but gangsters of the roaring Twenties actually saying something like this.
"How's tricks?"
"*Everything's jake*."
"Twenty-three skidoo!"

Ex

Universally understood verbal shorthand for Molson Export, the flagship beer of Molson Breweries. "I'll have a bottle of *Ex*, please."

exchange rate

The relative values of the Canadian and American dollars. For instance, the U.S. dollar is most often worth more than the Canadian dollar with the *exchange rate* being $1 Canadian for, say, $1.22 American. The exchange rate is often displayed on signs in convenience stores in large Canadian cities since American tourists often don't bother getting their money converted in the (sadly correct) belief that Canadian merchants will take their greenbacks.

E

Expulsion

The forcible removal of French Acadians by the British between 1755 and 1762. The Acadians found new homes throughout North America, particularly in Louisiana, where they became "cajuns."

face off
In hockey, the dropping of the puck to begin or resume play.

faller
In BC, a logger whose specific job is to actually cut down the trees. "I've moved up from *whistle punk* to *faller*."

farforth
In Newfoundland, a phrase meaning "as much as," "as far as" or "insofar as." "You can't be too careful so *farforth* as what dynamite's concerned. That's why they call me Lefty."

farmer's blessing
In PEI, snow in May, because it seeps down and waters the crops. "There's a *farmer's blessing* falling today so be careful on the roads." (See also *poor man's fertilizer*.)

Ferme ton gorlot!
In Québec, "Shut up!" (literally, "Stop ringing your sleighbell!")
"Then I went to the *dépanneur*, but they wouldn't

take my *Canadian Tire money* so I couldn't buy any *cretons* so I say to the clerk, *'Va pèter dans le trèfle,'* and then I—"

"Ferme ton gorlot!"

Fête nationale
In Québec, the official name of the holiday observed on June 24, but more commonly known as St. Jean Baptiste Day.

fèves au lard
French for "beans with pork." This is another phrase whose meaning is known to most *anglos* from its appearances on canned food labels. Like everywhere else in North America, the contents of such cans are actually beans in sauce with a microscopic particle of bacon rind floating around in it to justify the "with pork."

(a) few logs short of a full load
Especially appropriate for use in BC logging camps, this woodsy insult is the *lumberjack* equivalent of "a sandwich or two short of a picnic," "half a bubble off plumb," or "a few cents shy of a dollar." It means that the person referred to is slightly deficient in sanity, intelligence or good judgment—possibly all three. "Oh, that's Fir-brained Fred. When the trees fall, he tries to catch them. He's *a few logs short of a full load,* if you get my drift."

fiddlehead

The edible, tightly furled fronds of the ostrich fern *(Atteuccia struthiopteris)*, so-called because they resemble the carved scrollwork found at the end of a violin's neck. Boiled, *fiddleheads* are a traditional dish in Québec, Atlantic Canada and some New England states. In Canada, they have now achieved sporadic popularity all across the country.

fiddler

In Newfoundland, an accordion player. If Newfies once had a reputation for not having so much going on upstairs, surely colloquialisms like this didn't help.

"Go ask the *fiddler* for a tune."

"Where is he?"

"Right there!"

"I just see the accordion player."

"That's right, the *fiddler*. You *come from away, my son?*"

figgy duff

1) Especially in Newfoundland, a kind of boiled pudding containing raisins. In some English dialects, "fig" meant "raisin," and "duff" meant "dough." 2) The name of a folk-rock band from Newfoundland, mainly active in the 1970s and '80s. They travelled the *East Coast*, learning traditional songs and infusing them with rock and roll elements. *Figgy Duff* is seen to have played an

important part in popularizing Newfoundland culture during the years they were active.

Fin du Monde (End of the World)

The brand name of a potent kind of Belgian-style beer made in Québec (the coastal outline of which is glowingly featured on the label). Its name comes from the supposed belief of European explorers that, upon reaching Québec, they had arrived at the edge of the earth.

Finnegan

A floppy-eared dog puppet on the long-running children's TV show, *Mr. Dressup*. For more details, see *Casey and Finnegan*.

First Nations

The Aboriginal peoples of Canada, but not including the Inuit or *Métis*.

fish

In Newfoundland, *cod*. Of course, Newfoundlanders know that *fish* also has a generic meaning, but the odds are that if you're on *The Rock* and you hear people talk about *fish*, they specifically mean *cod*. Aside from that, it is worth noting that the *Dictionary of Newfoundland English* (cited as a reference for this book) contains eight pages of terms starting with the word "fish."

fishocracy

In 19th-century Newfoundland, 1) Wealthy

merchants who had profited from the fishing trade and were opposed to self-government. 2) The entire chain of people who made their living by the fishing trade, from the wealthiest merchant to the humblest fisherman.

"Here, we call our scaly betters the *fishocracy*."

"In Boston, we call them the cod-fish aristocracy."

"It's a bleedin' fishtatorship is what it is."

five-pin bowling

A slimmed down version of ten-pin bowling, played only in Canada and invented by Thomas Ryan in Toronto, circa 1908. Ryan ran a pool hall and a bowling alley. Ten-pin bowling was growing in popularity, but many of Ryan's customers found the 4.5-kilogram (10-pound) ball too heavy. Spotting an opportunity, Ryan came up with the five-pin version, featuring a smaller, lighter ball.

flatlander

In BC, 1) Someone from the Prairies, especially. 2) Someone from anywhere else in Canada. Think of it as the West Coast equivalent of *come from away*.

"What's this *Kokanee* stuff?"

"Hey, everybody, the *flatlander* wants to know what *Kokanee* is!"

float camp

1) A large log raft on which is built the living quarters for an entire logging crew. "Dear L.M.

Montgomery: Thank you for submitting your romance novella 'Two Years on a *Float Camp.*' Unfortunately, it does not meet our present needs. Might we recommend you make a foray into juvenile literature, for which there is a much greater demand?" 2) Sometimes today, a floating crew camp built on a foundation of industrially produced flotation materials. "Dear Ms. Montgomery: Thank you for submitting the script of your original television pilot '*Boom* Raider: The *Float Camp* Chronicles.' Might we suggest that you re-tool it into something we could call 'The FC' or maybe even, 'Anne of GG: Teen Super Shero'?"

F

flossy

Over embellished. "Your *cow's breakfast* is lookin' a bit *flossy* what with all those flowers and garlands and whatnot."

flower count

Since 1976, a yearly ritual that takes place in Victoria, BC, during February. To showcase their balmy climate while the rest of the country is still in the dead of winter, Victorians take to the streets and count all the flowers in bloom (with totals allegedly surpassing 100 million). This would seem to confirm Victoria's reputation as the *City of the Newly Wed and Nearly Dead*, since who but blushing brides and snow-haired retirees has the time or temperament to traipse around counting flowers?

flying axehandles

In PEI, diarrhea. "You can call it *back door trots* or you can call it *flying axehandles*. They're both *equal to me.*"

flying low

For trouser wearers, the unenviable state of the having your pants zipper (commonly known as "the fly") half, or completely, undone.

"People here are real friendly. Everybody I've passed in the street has smiled."

"'Cause you're *flyin' low* is why."

Flying Yesterday's Aircraft Today

The unofficial motto of the Canadian Forces Air Command, in reference to its famously outdated aircraft.

foot hockey

Not so much hockey as soccer played with a tennis ball.

forty-pounder

A 40-ounce bottle of liquor.

"Is that the sound of Chad *reconsidering lunch?*"

"Yeah, he drank most of a *forty-pounder* last night."

four by four

When ordering coffee, especially at *Tim Hortons*, to ask for four creams and four sugars. The inclusion of the term *four by four* in this dictionary should not be interpreted as endorsement of polluting one's coffee in this manner. Really, you are simply adding a dash of coffee to a syrupy compound of sugar and cream; you might as well let some ice cream melt and just pour the coffee into that. If *Tim Hortons* hasn't already come out with a drink like this, you heard it here first (see also *triple-triple*).

F

francophone

1) A French-speaking Canadian. "She's a *francophone*." 2) An adjective to describe French-speaking Canadians:
"The *francophone language police* are out in full force today."
"What other kind of *language police* are there?"

Franglais

1) Phrases that are a mixture of French and English, such as "Bon weekend." 2) The common use of a French or English word when speaking the other language: "Voulez vous un *hot dog?*" or "I'm going to the *dépanneur.*"

frazil

Slushy ice formed when water is not still enough to completely freeze. It comes from the French Canadian "frazil" for "snow floating in water," which in turn comes from the French "fraisil" for "cinders." "Looks like it's time to turn the furnace on. There's *frazil* in the toilet."

freeze-up

In the Prairies of yesteryear, the onset of winter, when cold conditions put an end to outdoor work for the winter. "*Freeze-up*'s upon us. Time to put on your *mackinaw* and take the equipment in."

Frenchman's turkey

In PEI, a fish dinner, usually herring.
"I eat *fish*, but not fowl. What do you recommend?"
"How about a nice plate of *Frenchman's turkey?*"

(The) Friendly Giant

A beloved children's TV program airing on the *CBC* from 1958 to 1985. The Giant (played by Bob Homme) was named "Friendly," and together with two puppets, Rusty the rooster and Jerome the giraffe, told simple stories and played songs. Memorable moments that occurred in every episode included Friendly's huge hand setting out miniature furniture for his guests (viewers) and a cow jumping over the moon as the program drew to a close. Both the show and its star were transplanted from Madison, Wisconsin, to find a happy and long-lasting home in Canada. By the end of its run, more than 3000 15-minute episodes of *The Friendly Giant* had been produced.

from away

In PEI, descriptive of someone from any place other than PEI or the Maritimes; a shorter version of *come from away*.

"I was wavin' goodbye and told him *'Don't let your antifreeze,'* and he just looks at me."
"What do you want. He's *from away.*"

front room
Especially in the Prairies and Maritimes, a term used to describe the sitting room, living room or so-called good room favoured by hosts for entertaining and by families for hanging out in. "The *front room* is where we keep all the doilies and antimacassars."

fruit rancher
In BC, the owner or operator of a fruit orchard. "The life of a *lumberjack* was not for him, so he packed it in and became a *fruit rancher.*"

fuddle duddle
When former Prime Minister Pierre Trudeau was accused of swearing during a parliamentary session, he responded that he had, in fact, said *fuddle duddle*, prompting one observer to quip, "The prime minister wishes to be obscene and not heard."

full Nanaimo
In 1970s BC, a mode of dress in the poorest of taste, consisting of white shoes, a shiny white belt of faux leather, polyester pants and a blazer with a phony crest. Apparently cities and towns substituted their rivals' names, so that, depending on where you were from, it might be known as "the full Kelowna" or "the full Penticton."

F

funny money

What visiting Americans habitually call Canadian paper currency because its denominations come in more colours than just sickly green. This writer vividly remembers going to an Ontario fair as a child and seeing a bellicose Texan in a Stetson, proudly displaying a squirrel whose life had been spent learning to water ski. Upon concluding the demonstration of his water-skiing squirrel, he had the temerity to turn to the audience and say, "One thing I've learned bein' up here in Canada is that you have *funny money*."

future strength

A polite way of saying that someone is no good at something, especially in the office or service industry. "Serving drinks without spilling them on the patrons' laps is one of her *future strengths*."

G

gaffer

In Newfoundland, a young boy capable of help-
ing older men at work. "Get one of them *gaffers*
away from their game of *steppycock* and get him to
untangle the nets."

Game ho!

In the early days of hockey, this was what players
said when they had scored a goal, although today
it sounds more like something you'd hear on
a foxhunt rather than at a hockey game.

Game on!

Heralds the resumption of play in *road hockey*
games. After calling *"Car!"* and moving the net
out of the way, the players wait for the car to go
by, then move the *net* back into position and call,
"Game on!" This is the signal for everyone to start
swatting at the tennis ball again.

gaufres

French for "waffles" and known to many English-
speaking Canadians from frozen waffle packaging.
This term comes from the French for "honeycomb"

and refers here to the criss-cross patterns on waffles. It is also the root of "gopher," stemming from the time when early French settlers noticed the elaborate tunnel systems of the New World's indigenous ground squirrels.

gaunch/gitch/gotch/gotchies

Underwear. "Whose *gaunch* is this all over the living room?" or "Pack up your *gitch* and get out of my house" or "If you don't have any clean *gotch*, there's no way you're wearing any of mine" or "Fell in the lake? Well, strip down to your *gotchies* and dry out the rest of your clothes by the fire."

geoduck (pron: GOOey-duck)

Especially in BC, a kind of burrowing clam (*Panope generosa*) with a sucking siphon of decidedly penile appearance. Its prowess at burying itself in sludgy river bottoms, however, is not enough to prevent humans from digging up and eating it in great numbers.

"Have you ever tried *geoduck?*"

"You're offering me a sticky mallard?"

get to blanket harbour

In PEI, to go to bed. "Well, it's been a *large day*. Time to *get to blanket harbour*."

giants of the Prairies

A series of large roadside attractions in the Prairies. The *giants of the Prairies* are usually erected near small towns with the intent of making tourists stop to take pictures and, presumably, to buy *chocolate bars* and *pop* in town, thus stimulating the local economy. They include the *Big Perogie*, the Giant *Pysanka*, a *ginormous kubasa* and various kinds of wild animals. The signs alerting drivers to their proximity almost always start with "World's Largest...."

ginormous (pron: jy-NOR-mus)

Really big.

"Look at that *ginormous* badminton racket by the side of the road!"

"The sign says it's the world's largest."

"That must mean we're in St. Albert, Alberta."

"Let's stop and take pictures and buy *pop* and *chocolate bars.*"

give 'er

To undertake an activity with the utmost enthusiasm. Apparently this stems from an old logging camp phrase, "Give her *snoose*," which more or less meant "Have at it with everything you've got" (puzzlingly, *snoose* is *Chinook jargon* for "chewing tobacco"). "Everybody ready? On the count of three—*give 'er!*"

Glooscap

A legendary demi-god of the Micmac and Malecite *First Nations*. He is revered as a mighty warrior and magician.

glory fit

In Newfoundland, a lively show of religious enthusiasm.

"Is your mother having a conniption of some sort?"

"Naw, it's just a *glory fit.*"

go down the road

1) In the Maritimes, to leave the East Coast in search of employment. "Well, *my son,* you're a man now and it's time to *go down the road.*"

2) With the substitution of "Goin'" for "go" the name of an iconic 1970 Canadian film about two Maritimers who go to Toronto in search of a better life. The film was masterfully spoofed by *SCTV.*

Go Leafs, Go!

The brainless exhortation of Toronto's hockey zombies to their blue-garbed masters.

go to the washroom

To defecate or urinate, even when there is no actual washroom in sight; for example, when camping, "I really need to *go to the washroom.*"

goal suck

A hockey player who hovers around the opposing team's *net* in the hopes of scoring.

gone to the sand hills

In Alberta, to be dead.

"How's that 19-year-old cat of yours?"

"*Gone to the sand hills.*"

good, good whole wheat Shreddies

A memorable advertising jingle for *Shreddies* cereal, this phrase has been seared into the collective unconscious of Canadians.

(a) good head for bouncing bricks off

Those of less than average intelligence shouldn't be surprised to hear this when doing something dumb in PEI. "When the door handle reads 'Push,' she pulls. She's got *a good head for bouncing bricks off.*"

G

Gordie Howe hat trick

In hockey, to score a goal, get an *assist* and get into a fight all in the same game.

Great White North

1) A humorous way of referring to Canada, popularized in the early 1980s by the *McKenzie Brothers*. 2) The name of the *McKenzie Brothers'* TV segment, which, in its definitive form, featured Bob and Doug sitting in front of a map of Canada, dressed in parkas and *tuques*, drinking beer out of *stubbies* and discussing a succession of inane topics. "Welcome to the *Great White North, eh?* Today's topic is the *metric system.*"

green hornets

In Ottawa and Toronto of the 1960s and 1970s, municipal employees who gave out parking tickets. Although everyone agrees that the nickname came in part from their green uniforms, some say the "hornet" was because of the buzzing sound their motorcycles made, while others say it was because of the "stinging" fines they imposed.

green jellybean day

A wartime ruse invented by BC's navy seamen for use upon returning home from long voyages. Dads would greet their kids at the front door and then scatter a bag of green jellybeans on the verdant lawn. In those simpler, pesticide-free times, this gave Mum and Dad some time alone together while their progeny searched for the jellybeans. Said one returning father, "The trick is to toss out 99 and tell them there's a hundred."

Grey Cup

1) A trophy that is the holy grail of the CFL. 2) The football game played for this trophy, usually in November. "Are you watching the *Grey Cup* on the weekend?"

grounds

In Newfoundland, an expanse of water where commercial fishing is sanctioned or practiced. "These are the best fishing *grounds* for miles." "Why aren't they called fishing **waters** instead?" "Because they're called *grounds*."

(The) Group of Seven

An influential cadré of impressionist landscape painters active as a group from 1920 to 1931 and as individuals long after that. Focussed mainly on wilderness and arctic scenes, the *Group of Seven* were the first to effectively embody a Canadian school of art. Although to some extent ridiculed at the outset, their paintings are renowned today as visceral reflections of Canada's natural beauty, sometimes joyous, sometimes melancholy, but always worthy of appreciation. Members were Franklin Carmichael (1890–1945), Lawren Harris (1885–1970), A.Y. Jackson (1882–1974), Frank Johnston (1888–1949), Arthur Lismer (1885–1969), J.E.H. MacDonald (1873–1932) and Frank Varley (1881–1969). Emily Carr (1871–1945) and Tom Thompson (1877–1917) were associated with the *Group of Seven* but were never actually members.

grow-op
Short for "growing operation," meaning a commercially maintained marijuana plantation. It could just as easily stand for "grow opportunity" since grow-operatives can be very creative in where they set up shop, perhaps the most ambitious being throughout a massive abandoned brewery just north of Toronto. Usually, though, they are in homes.
"Have you got a darkroom in your closet?"
"Naw, it's my *grow-op*."

guignolée
In some parts of Québec, on New Year's Eve, young men go from door to door, singing carols and collecting money for the poor—this custom is called la *guignolée*.

gullywasher

In PEI, a very heavy rain. Overheard between three friends, one of them *from away*.

"It's a real *blueberry run* today."

"Yup—a proper *gully washer*."

"Why can't you people just say 'rain'?"

Gyproc

A brand name of drywall, being a combination of "gypsum" and "rock." However, in the same way that the brand name Kleenex has come to refer to any disposable tissue, *Gyproc* is often used to describe any kind of drywall regardless of brand affiliation. "We need three more sheets of *Gyproc* to finish this wall."

H

habitant (pron: a-bee-TONH)

1) Up until the early 20th century, a French settler in Québec, sometimes used in a pejorative sense like "redneck" or "yokel," but later reclaimed and worn proudly. 2) When capitalized, a brand name of hearty canned soup, especially pea.

Habs

The nickname given to the Montréal Canadiens hockey team, in reference to the mistaken belief that the "H" in the "HC" logo on players' jerseys stands for *habitant*. The entire logo really stands for "Club de Hockey Canadien." Nonetheless, the name has stuck and most Québecers will pronounce it "layz Abs."

Haida

A *First Nation* group whose members live primarily in BC's Queen Charlotte Islands. The *Haida* are renowned for their beautiful sculpting of wood, silver, argillite and gold.

hairy canary

A fit of temper. "Don't have a *hairy canary*." (See also *rangy*.)

hand socks

In BC, PEI and elsewhere this means "mittens," especially oversized or clumsy ones.

"What are you doing behind that tree? You said you needed to *drain the main vein*."

"I do, but these *hand socks* are making it tricky to get my fly open."

"Then take them off for a minute."

"Oh, I hadn't thought of that."

handy

In Newfoundland, to be nearby, especially geographically. "We'll be there soon. My secret fishing *grounds* are *handy*."

hangashore

In Newfoundland, a weak, sickly or unfortunate person. The expression comes **not** from the idea of someone so unwell they must stay on land instead of going to sea, but rather from the Irish expression "angishore," meaning an unfortunate or pitiable wretch.

"Did you hear that Bob's got rickets, hemorrhoids and *flying axehandles?*"

"The poor *hangashore*."

hangin' kill

In Ontario's southwestern tobacco belt, this means "hanging kiln"—that is, to hang racks of newly picked tobacco leaves in a kiln to be dried. As such it is the name of a specific job once performed by labourers, now often accomplished through automation.

"Got a job for the summer?"

"Hangin' kill. You?"

"Shakin' stick."

(The) Happy Gang

A lunchtime radio variety show that aired on the *CBC* from 1937 to 1959. Starting in the depths of the Great Depression, Canadians could tune in for a bit of noontime levity as a small orchestra played lighthearted songs mixed with banter, comedic skits and other humorous routines. For 22 years, listeners would hear the sound of a knock at the door, followed by "Who's there?" and several voices replying in unison, *"The Happy Gang!"* The first voice replied, "Well, come onnnnn in!"

hard done by

Describes someone harshly or unfairly treated. "Ever since we told the whole town that Bob has rickets, hemorrhoids and *flying axehandles*, he's feeling sort of *hard done by*."

hat trick

In hockey, the scoring of three goals in one game by the same player, at which point the fans throw their hats on to the ice in celebration. In the late 1940s, Sammy Taft, a Toronto haberdasher, made a bet with Alex Kaleta, a visiting player from the Chicago Blackhawks; if Kaleta could score three goals against the Leafs that night, Taft would give him a free hat. Kaleta kept his part of the bargain. So did Taft. And the rest is hockey history.

(to) have had the biscuit

To be done for, dead, no good for anything. Overheard at the roadside:
"Do you think you could give me a lift into town? My car's *had the biscuit*."
"You're right. *There's nowhere that'll go in a day*."

HBC

The Hudson's Bay Company. Founded on May 2, 1670, *HBC* is the oldest commercial corporation in North America and one of the oldest in the world. At one time it was the largest private landowner in Canada and the de facto government in many areas. As such, the letters *HBC* are also jokingly taken to mean "Here Before Christ" and also "Hungry Belly Company." *HBC*'s current retail outlets are simply referred to as "The Bay."

he couldn't beat up a carload of poets

Said of someone who is very weak. In many ways the polar opposite of *eat sawdust and shit two-by-fours*. "That *hangashore couldn't beat up a carload of poets*."

he doesn't have his stick on the ice

While it stems from hockey jargon, in everyday conversation, this expression describes someone behaving erratically, frantically or unstably.
"Did you hear Bob's latest plan? He wants to go into business selling dehydrated water."
"*He doesn't have his stick on the ice*."

He shoots! He scores!

A phrase coined by Canada's pioneer of hockey commentating, Foster Hewitt. If you were a kid growing up anywhere in Canada during the 1970s, this phrase was unavoidable and could be used for anything from actually scoring a goal in street hockey to congratulating one's self on a jape or antic well done, such as giving someone a wedgie.

H

He went for a dump and the gophers got him

On the Prairies, this is a colourful way of saying that someone has gotten lost.

"Where's Uncle Norm? He was supposed to meet us here at one o'clock."

"He went for a dump and the gophers got him."

health card

The plastic identification card that opens the doors of Canada's universal health system. Some people have the old model with the horizontal bands of red and white, while others have the more up-to-date green version with the bearer's photo. The seven words most often heard by Canadians making doctors' appointments are, "Make sure you bring your *health card.*"

heritage moments

1) A series of short, interstitial films depicting significant events from Canada's history and officially called "Historica Minutes." Generally

60 seconds long, they were introduced in 1991 and have been aired by various broadcasters. Seventy-four strong at the time of this writing, they depict events ranging from the execution of Louis Riel to the creation of Superman. Not surprisingly, they count towards broadcasters' *CanCon* quotas. Popular at first, their ubiquity, earnest tone and sometimes cheesy sentiments have led some to call them "Heritage McMoments." They are frequently spoofed by Canadian comedians and filmmakers. 2) The phrase can also be used to describe an event (of national or intimate scope) found to be moving by some but not others: "Oh, look, he's proposing to her by karaoke and singing 'You Light Up My Life.' Ain't that a *heritage moment.*"

herring choker

Maritime slang for 1) Someone from the Maritimes. 2) Someone from New Brunswick.
"Three *Canucks* walk into a bar. One's *Québecois*, one's a *flatlander* and the third is a *herring choker.*"
"I've heard this one before."

high muckymuck/mucketymuck

A big shot; someone of importance, possibly obnoxious. This phrase comes from the *Chinook jargon* term "hiyu (great, much, big) muckamuck (food, to eat)." Anyone with lots of food was presumably well-off; that is, a person of means and substance.

"What's this stage and these flags and that microphone for?"

"Some *high mucketymuck* from *Ottawa*'s givin' a speech today."

"I smell a barnful of *CanCon* headed our way."

Hinterland Who's Who

A series of interstitial film segments about wildlife, produced by Environment Canada and airing primarily during the 1960s and '70s, but revived in 2003. Each segment featured soothing flute music and the mellifluous tones of an announcer describing fascinating facts about Canada's indigenous wildlife as well as information about conservation. *Hinterland Who's Who* has been affectionately spoofed by various comedians and filmmakers.

(l')hivernants

Voyageurs who paddled any route during the winter months, as opposed to their less hardy *mangeurs de lard* colleagues.

Hockey Night in Canada (a.k.a. "HNIC," "Hockey Fight in Canada," and so forth)

A long-running *CBC* television program that broadcasts two hockey games every Saturday night. With its origin in a series of 1931 radio broadcasts, *Hockey Night in Canada* moved to TV in 1952 and has been on the air ever since. Its theme (*Da da da DAH da DAH!*) has been called Canada's second national anthem. Its current host, the stoic

Ron MacLean, is frequently joined for "Coach's Corner" segments by the loud-spoken and even louder-clad Don Cherry.

hockey widow

Any woman whose partner is frequently absent because of playing hockey (either professionally or at an amateur level), watching hockey (either professionally or at an amateur level) or talking about hockey (either professionally or at an amateur level). *Hockey widows* are especially common during *playoffs*.

Hogtown

Toronto. This term may have come about because of early Toronto's teeming farmers' market with its attendant livestock, or it may have been in reference to the fact that the rest of the country once felt (and still feels) that Toronto takes everything for itself, which is only right what with it being the *centre* of the universe and all. Overheard in the Maritimes:

"You planning to *go down the road* to *Hogtown?*"

"Nope. *Hong-Kouver.*"

holubtsi

On the Prairies, cabbage rolls (Ukrainian, pron: HOL-up-chee). "When you're done cleaning the Giant *Pysanka*, come and have a nice plate of *holubtsi.*"

Holy jumpin'

An exclamation of surprise, possibly as a less blasphemous version of "Holy Jesus!"
"Did you see where Pat gave up his fishin' *grounds* and became a *fruit rancher* out west?"
"Holy jumpin'!"

homme du nord

French for "man of the north," in this case being either a synonym for a *voyageur*, or in some cases, specifically a *voyageur* who worked through the winter as opposed to paddling an easier route during the cold months.

Hong-Kouver

Vancouver, because of its large numbers of immigrants from the Pacific Rim.
"Next quiz question: Who can tell me what Canadian city has the highest vertical population density in the world outside of Japan?"
"Hong-Kouver."
"That is not an acceptable answer."
"Uh…*Van Groovy?*"
"No!"
"Mmmm—how about *Lotus Land?*"
"I'll accept that."

Honourable Member

1) A formal title for members of parliament, usually followed by the name of the member's riding. "Would the *Honourable Member* from Mount Royal care to spell *fuddle duddle?*" 2) Slang

for penis. "I must allow my *Honourable Member* to pass water" (which should go to show non-Canadians how seriously we take our politics).

hoodoo

Unusually shaped pillars found on the Prairies. Formed from soft sedimentary rock protected by a cap of harder rock on top, *hoodoos* were eroded into their present shapes by wind and the other elements. They are found throughout the U.S. *as well* and called by the same name. In Canada, they were once known also as "demoiselles." In the legends of North American Aboriginal cultures, a "hoodoo" is a bad omen or evil spirit.

hooktender

In logging lore of yesteryear, the *hooktender* was the person whose job it was to secure a large load of logs together, ready for hauling. Once the logs were securely bundled together, the *hooktender* sent a signal to the *whistle punk* who then blew his whistle to alert the *donkeyman* that he could start the engine to haul the logs.

hoot and holler and wave your donut

In PEI, "Go ahead and celebrate wildly."
"I've just won the lottery!"
"Go *hoot and holler and wave your donut!*"

horse bun

In rural areas, a piece of horse manure. Overheard between a country cousin and city cousin, not the best of friends:

"Care to try a *horse bun?*"
"Sure, put it right here on my plate."

hoser

1) An insult basically equivalent to "loser" but also suggesting "idiot," "goof," and so on. It seems to come from the term "to hose," which was once a vulgar way of referring to the male's role during sex. It was then transferred into the sporting arena to mean "to take advantage of, treat unfairly or defeat convincingly." For instance, "The *Leafs* got hosed by the *Habs.*" In this sense it may also refer to a supposed tradition in which the losing team had to hose off the ice. 2) A description of an uncouth, plaid shirt-wearing, beer-drinking, hockey-watching male as personified by the *McKenzie Brothers*.

hot arse

In Newfoundland, a kind of kettle with a flat bottom causing it to heat up very quickly. Unfortunately, for those not in the know, this expression can cause problems by turning the most innocent domestic compliment into a hunka hunka salacious innuendo.

"I was just admiring your *hot arse.*"
"I've always liked you too."
"Er…I was really just hoping for a cup of tea."

hot dog

That shameful but pervasive English term that Québecers usually pronounce as "ott-dog", much to the annoyance of the *language police*. Referring to a *hot dog* as a "chien chaud" (the literal and technically correct term) will immediately tell everyone you are not from Québec.

"Un chien chaud s'il vous plait?"

"You want an *'ot dog*? Not from around here are you?"

How's it goin'?

"How are you?" or "How are things?" While it was already a casual and commonplace platitude beforehand, in the early 1980s, the *McKenzie Brothers* gave this phrase an undeniable boost in popularity when their TV appearances and hit record spawned a generation of teenage boys who thought nothing of greeting everyone they met with a ubiquitous, *"How's it goin', eh?"*

How's your belly button?/feet and ears?/ old straw hat?

A nonsense greeting sometimes heard in PEI, meaning simply, "How are you doing?"

"How's your belly button?"

"Oh, fair to middling."

(Note: In the Upper Ottawa Valley, a variation of this goes: "How's yer belly where the pig bit ya?" The appropriate response: "All healed up now with the hair growin' on it!")

humdurgin

In BC logging-speak of yore, a self-propelled, log-unloading vehicle once used by Comox Logging and Railway Co.

Husky station

One of 500 filling stations across Canada owned by Husky Energy Inc. Along with signs showing a husky dog, *Husky stations* are notable for the giant Canadian flags that many of them fly. Most locations are a combination of filling station and family restaurant, making them popular with both professional truck drivers and vacationers. In parts of Western Canada, they are branded, "Mohawk Gas."

"We haven't eaten for hours, we're exhausted, the kids have to *go to the washroom*, we're desperately in need of fuel and we're hours from anywhere—what are we going to do?"

"Look! It's a *Husky station*!"

"Oh, thank goodness!"

hyack/hyak

Chinook jargon. 1) An imperative command meaning "Hurry up!" "*Hyak, Cheechako!*" 2) An adjective for "quickly" or "fast." "Get your *chic chic* hitched up *hyak*."

hyas

Chinook jargon. "Big" or "much." "Your town is *hyas kloosh*."

hyas tyee

Chinook jargon. "Big chief" or "important person."

"She's a real *hyas tyee*."

H

"A *high mucketymuck* you might say?"
"No, nicer than that."

hydro

1) Any provincial supplier of electricity (from "hydroelectric"; that is, electricity produced by controlled water flow, although most utilities so-called have long included coal-fired and nuclear power). "Oh man, BC *Hydro* turned off the power because I'm late with the bill." 2) Electricity itself. "Oh man, they've turned the *hydro* off because I didn't pay my bill." 3) Short for "hydroponic" marijuana. Sure to cause confusion in cases where its meaning may be mistaken for that of hydro-electricity.

"I've got some great BC *hydro*."
"How can that be when we're in Ontario? They let you bring it with you?"

I don't care if school keeps or not

In PEI, an expression of indifference.

"Do you prefer to call it *back door trots* or *flying axehandles?*"

"*I don't care if school keeps or not.*"

I wouldn't wear that to a dogfight

A phrase not heard nearly often enough and used to describe a particularly ugly piece of clothing. Overheard in the head of a soon-to-be brides-maid: "Mustard-coloured crinoline? *I wouldn't wear that to a dogfight!*"

ice hole

1) A hole cut through the surface ice of a frozen lake and used for ice fishing. 2) An insult that is technically not swearing, but certainly sounds like it. "Don't be such an *ice hole.*"

ice palace

A hockey arena.

ice pan

A thick sheet or substantial slab of floating ice.

"The rules of *steppycock* are simple. You follow the

leader, who jumps from one *ice pan* to another. The first one to fall in loses."

"I'll say."

icing sugar

Finely powdered sugar used in baking, especially to make icing for cakes and other treats. *South of the border,* it is called "powdered sugar" or "confectioner's sugar."

idiot mittens

Children's mittens connected by an *idiot string*.

idiot stick

In BC, a carved gewgaw of supposedly Aboriginal provenance sold to willingly gullible tourists, usually representing totem poles. Overheard in a Vancouver souvenir shop:

"How're sales this morning?"

"I sold three plush *Mounties,* five plastic *inukshuks* and about a million *idiot sticks.*"

idiot string

A once-popular way of preventing children's mittens from becoming lost by tying them together with a string that ran through both sleeves of the child's coat so that one mitten would hang down from the end of each sleeve. Like most other things that are either useful or fun, they have since been discouraged because they are considered choking hazards.

igloo

A dome-shaped *Inuit* shelter built of snow blocks and considered by some to be emblematic of Canada. According to most Canadians, "Americans think we all live in *igloos*." This perception got a boost in credibility when Canadian comedian Rick Mercer famously got Arkansas governor and subsequent presidential hopeful Mike Huckabee to congratulate Canada for building a protective dome over our "national igloo." (Mercer also convinced Americans that, among other things, Canada classified golden retrievers as elephants so they could not be used for hard labour.)

I'm in no mood for an organ recital

A useful phrase for women tired of hearing their male friends brag about sexual conquests.

in his cups

Drunk.

"Is Fred playing *road hockey* with a *pecker pole* again?"

"What do you want? He's *in his cups*."

in the toolies

In BC especially, 1) To be in a remote location, comparable to going to the *back forty*.

"What happened to you?"

"Sorry, I got lost *in the toolies*."

2) To have accidentally driven off the road.

"Well, we're *in the toolies* now."

"Do you mind rolling up your window so the cows can't stick their heads in?"

INCO

Formerly, the International Nickel Company Ltd. *INCO* today is a wholly owned subsidiary of the Brazilian mining company, Vale. It did, and still does, employ substantial numbers of Canadians in mining, smelting and exploration. It was immortalized in the *Stompin' Tom* song, "Sudbury Saturday Night." "Oh, the girls are out to bingo / and the boys are gettin' stinko / and we'll think no more of *INCO* / on a Sudbury Saturday night."

Inuit

An Inuktitut word meaning literally "men" or "people" and the name by which the Aboriginal and cultural groups formerly known to *kablunas* as "Eskimos" generally refer to themselves. It should be noted that Inuit is the plural form, with "Inuk" being the singular, meaning "man" or "person" (see *inukshuk*). This term is preferred in Canada and Greenland, where "Eskimo" is considered offensive by some. However, some related groups in Alaska and Siberia prefer to use the term "Eskimo" which, for them, includes both the Yupik and Inupiat peoples.

inukshuk (pron: in-NOOK-shook)

A human-shaped figure made from stacked, balanced stones. The name is Inuktitut for "acting in the capacity of a man" ("inuk" means "man").

Initially called "inunguaks" ("like a man"), they probably first served as ceremonial appeals to the gods for good hunting and were placed at key routes along the migratory routes of caribou. Later, they came to serve as navigational beacons in a terrain devoid of trees or other easily recognizable landmarks. They could also be used to indicate good hunting grounds. In modern culture they have evolved into propitious symbols of human welcome and assistance in a sometimes harsh environment. They have come to symbolize both the warmth and hardiness of Canadians as a whole.

"Is that an *inukshuk* up ahead?"

"No, it's that frozen *kabluna* from last year who went for a swim then climbed out and waved at us. Remember?"

Iqaluit

The territorial capital of *Nunavut*, previously named Frobisher Bay. With a population of just over 6000, it is Canada's least populous capital city.

Irish moss

In PEI, an edible kind of seaweed related to dulse. As well as being considered a delicacy on its own, it can be used as a stabilizer for commercially prepared foods and as such provides an important source of employment for many Islanders.

I

I'se the By

A traditional Newfoundland folk song, whose title means "I'm the boy." Although it celebrates the boisterous, rollicking good times of building boats and catching fish in Newfoundland, the song itself can be a source of dismay to Canadian school children who are made to sing it by well-intentioned but misguided teachers. Its repeated and enforced singing can be an emotionally scarring experience for 10-year-olds previously innocent of the names, "Fogo," "Twillingate," "Moreton's Harbour" and, of course, who could forget "Bonavista." It is also the first cause that most Canadians have to find out what a "petticoat" is and why it should want a border.

It may not be the end of the world, but you can see it from there

A phrase describing some forsaken and, presumably uninviting, remote location.
"Where's this wedding that we have to go to on the weekend?"
"Way out on the *back forty in the toolies. It may not be the end of the world, but you can see it from there.*"

It's better than a kick in the ass with a frozen boot

A phrase that can be used to describe something ranging from moderately good to quite excellent. (See also *better than a slap on the belly with a dead fish.*)

jambuster

In Manitoba and northwest Ontario, a sugar-coated, jam-filled donut.

"Can I get a *jambuster,* please?"

"You mean a *bismarck?*"

"I mean a freakin' *jelly doughnut* already."

"Then why didn't you just say so?"

Javex

A brand of liquid bleach. The name derives from "eau de javel," Javelle being the village in France where a solution of sodium hypochlorite was first used as bleach.

(the) Jaw

A nickname for Moose Jaw, Saskatchewan.

"What are you doing for the weekend?"

"Goin' to *the Jaw* to see my parents."

J-Cloth

A brand of reusable, absorbent cleaning cloths. They come in yellow, blue and pink. If you have Americans visiting and, for some reason, you send them out for cleaning products, you can have a bit of fun with them.

"Can you please pick up some *Javex* and *J-Cloths* while you're out."

"Do all the cleaning products in Canada start with the letter 'J'?"

Jean Baptiste

A fictional personification of French Canadians, usually portrayed as wearing a blue or red stocking cap such as we fondly imagine *voyageurs* might have worn.

jelly doughnut

A jelly-filled *doughnut* covered with icing sugar, seemingly called by a different name in almost every part of Canada.

"Can I get a *jelly doughnut* please?"

"You mean a *jambuster*."

"For God's sake, just give me a *jelly doughnut*."

"A *bismarck?*"

"Never mind. Instead, can I get a coffee with two cyanides and one strychnine?"

"Is that to go?"

"No, I'll drink it here."

jigging for cod

1) A method of catching *cod* without bait. Instead, a weighted hook is attached to a line and then repeatedly jerked sharply upwards. 2) A method of catching salmon barehanded when they are sluggish from spawning. It generally involves lowering one hand into the water and wiggling

your fingers like seaweed. In England, it was once a difficult but effective way of catching eels.

JK

In Ontario, Junior Kindergarten, for children ages four to five. Not all municipalities offer two levels of kindergarten, but some have both *JK* and SK (*Senior Kindergarten*).

joe job

Menial or monotonous employment, but often spoken of fondly by beleaguered executives or other people beset by the pressures of their jobs. "I'm gonna quit and go get some nice simple *joe job*." (*Joe jobs* can include being a waiter/waitress, bartender, janitor, truck driver, taxi driver, or selling fruit from a roadside stand, and so on.)

Johnny Canuck

1) A personification of English-speaking Canada, usually portrayed as wearing a hat roughly similar to a *Mountie*'s (for French Canada, see *Jean Baptiste*). 2) A Canadian soldier in either of the two world wars; in this case, roughly equivalent to the use of "G.I. Joe" in reference to U.S. soldiers.

Jos. Louis

A popular, cellophane-wrapped sweet treat made in Québec and consisting of a layer of vanilla paste, sandwiched between two circular chocolate layers of cake and then coated in a thin layer of flakey chocolate. They were invented in 1928 by baker Arcade Vachon and his wife, Rose Anna, who named their new confection "gâteau Jos. Louis" in honour of their two sons, Joseph and Louis. When spoken aloud, the name was then anglicized to "Joe Louie" although "Jos. Louis" still appears on the package. Asking visiting Americans to pick one up at the store is sure to inspire zany hilarity.

"Can you get me a *Jos. Louis* while you're out?"

"It's pronounced 'Lewis,' and I don't see how I could possibly bring you the former world heavyweight champion when he's been deceased for several years now."

joual

Working-class Canadian French considered to be uncouth because of its irregular syntax, dubious pronunciation and words borrowed from English. It comes from the French pronunciation of "cheval" for "horse," which was incorporated into the phrase "parler cheval" or "to speak badly." In use in France during the 19th century, in the 1950s it came to be applied to the distinctive sound of Québecois French.

jug milk

1) A phrase used to describe milk sold in reusable plastic jugs or recyclable cardboard cartons instead of clear plastic bags such as it is in Canada and

Europe. While plastic jugs are less and less common, this phrase was once used frequently to distinguish the kind of container you wanted your milk to come in. 2) In Ontario, sometimes used in reference to the actual convenience store where milk is purchased.

jus d'ananas

French for "pineapple juice" and included herein because it is yet another term that even the most die-hard *anglo* will recognize from the French side of food product packaging.

"Look at this. It contains sodium benzoate hydroxide and *jus d'ananas*."

J

just watch me

A phrase famously uttered by Pierre Trudeau during the *October Crisis*. When asked by a TV reporter how far he would go to restore order in a Québec shaken by political kidnappings, with the cameras rolling, Trudeau replied, "Well, *just watch me*." Three days later he invoked the War Measures Act and imposed martial law in parts of Québec. The phrase has since been used or referenced frequently in Canadian politics.

K

kabloona/kabluna

Inuktitut for "person with big eyebrows" or simply "the big eyebrow," specifically in reference to white Europeans.

"Why do you call them *kablunas*?"

"Because their eyebrows stick out like sun visors."

kamik

An Inuit boot, traditionally made from *caribou* or sealskin.

"The *kabluna beulahed* all over my new *kamiks!*"

Katimavik

(from Inuktitut for "meeting place") A federally funded youth volunteer program in some ways analogous to a domestic version of the U.S. Peace Corps initiative. Youth who apply are randomly selected from all across Canada and then sent on a nine-month excursion to participate in public works and social learning at various locations across the country. They are paid $3 a day and given $1000 if they complete the program. Founded in 1977, *Katimavik* peaked in the mid-1980s, when there were 5000 participants in any given year. Some disgruntled former participants have termed themselves "katimaviktims."

keener

Anyone, especially a student, who is either genuinely or falsely enthusiastic, attentive, proactive or involved.

"Wow, Susie's a real *keener*. She wrote the lesson plan on the board and drew up the seating arrangement."

"Well, she's the teacher, right? That's her job."

"Umm...actually, Susie's a student."

kerfuffle

A fuss or commotion, used in everyday conversation but also appropriate for specific circumstances.

Overheard between two hockey commentators:

"Don, would you say that this commotion on the ice is a *bench-clearing brawl?*"

"Ron, I wouldn't even call it a donnybrook."

"A *brouhaha* then?"

"Ron, it's barely a *kerfuffle*. I wish the refs would just let these guys play instead of blowing the whistle every time somebody gets shot—it's all part of the game. People are going to get hurt."

kétaine (pron: kay-TEN)

In Québec, kitschy, in poor taste.

"Inscribing your wedding invitations en *joual* was vraiment *kétaine*."

"Go practice your *Franglais* on somebody else."

K

ketchup-flavoured chips

Along with *Arborite*, *Coffee Crisp*, *J-Cloths*, milk in bags, *Smarties* and a host of others, *ketchup chips* are a uniquely Canadian consumer product.

keystone province

Manitoba, because of its shape on maps, seems to lock the other provinces together like a keystone.

kickwillee

Chinook jargon for "underneath." "Check out the *cheechako kickwillee* his *cultus chic chic*."

Kids in the Hall

1) A notorious sketch comedy troupe popular from the late 1980s through to the present. 2) Their eponymous TV show, which aired in Canada from 1988 to 1994. The *Kids in the Hall* have been called Canada's Monty Python by some, not least for their use of surrealist humour and drag. Some of their favourite subjects were big business, gay culture, youth subculture and seemingly "normal" family units.

King of Kensington

A TV sitcom that ran on *CBC* from 1975 to 1980 chronicling the misadventures of Larry King (played by Al Waxman), who owned a variety store in Toronto's Kensington Market neighbourhood. The show featured a multicultural cast reflective of Kensington's make-up at the time. Along with the apparently never-ending *Beachcombers*, *King of Kensington* is arguably the *CBC*'s best-known English comedy or drama from the 1970s. Its cultural influence has proven to be long and lasting. Singer, bandleader and personality Jaymz Bee not only formed the Al Waxman Fan Club in the late 1980s but also wrote and performed songs about *King of Kensington*. And today, there stands, or rather sits, a brown metal statue of Waxman on a park bench in the middle of present-day Kensington Market.

kittardy

In PEI, person of dubious mental acuity; in short, a half-wit. "How many times do I have to tell you—when I ask, *'How's your belly button?'* it's just a figure of speech. You don't actually have to pull up your shirt and look, ya big *kittardy*."

Klahanie

1) *Chinook jargon* for "outside" or "outdoors."
2) The name of a *CBC* television show that ran from 1967 to 1978, which focused on (surprise, surprise) wilderness and conservation.

Klahowya

Chinook jargon for "How are you?" "*Klahowya, cheechako*," or for those interested in Chinook/Inuktitut tongue-twisters, "*Klahowya, kabluna*."

Klondike

A region of the Yukon Territory containing the Klondike River and its tributaries. It was the scene of a gold rush in the late 1890s, and its legend looms large in Canada's sense of self-identity.

kloosh

Chinook jargon for "good" or "correct." "When things are bad between two friends, someone has to make them *kloosh*."

knuckle picker

In PEI, a person who removes the meat from lobsters' knuckles and arms. "Dear Sir or Madam: I have just come back *from away* where I worked *shakin' stick* and *hangin' kill*. I would now like to apply for gainful employment with your firm as a *knuckle picker*."

Kokanee

A brand of beer brewed and largely consumed in BC, with some popularity in other western provinces as well as the northwestern U.S. *Kokanee*'s principal tagline is "It's the beer out here."

kokum/kookum

"Grandmother" in some Cree dialects. "Come on, it's time to go and see your *kokum*."

Koo-loo-koo-koo-koo-loo-koo-KOO

The theme from *Bob and Doug McKenzie's Great White North* TV segments as seen on *SCTV*. It was hummed at the beginning of each episode by

Doug, played by Dave Thomas. Thomas has asserted in interviews that it was based on the flute music heard at the beginning of *Hinterland Who's Who*. In the early 1980s, it could also be heard in school corridors hummed by mainly *lumber jacket*-clad boys besotted with their *hoser* heroes.

Kraft Dinner/KD

Packaged macaroni and cheese made by Kraft. It is important to note that although it is available in both Canada and the U.S., only in Canada is it labelled *Kraft Dinner*; in the U.S., it is "Kraft Macaroni and Cheese." Canadians seem to be more likely to eat it as a dish unto itself as opposed to Americans who quite sensibly treat it as the grim sidedish that it is. Because it is cheap, usually costing less than a dollar for a box, *KD* has long been a staple in the diets of students and young people who either can't afford or can't be bothered to get a real meal together.

kubasa (pron: keel-BOSS-a)

From the Ukrainian for sausage, "kovbasa," kubasa is a garlic sausage popularized by the Ukrainian Canadian community. Similar words for the same foodstuff also appear in Polish. While the word is not used exclusively in Canada, *kubasa* is emblematic of the transplanted experience common to so many of Canada's European immigrants. "Every Saturday my mother goes to the *kubasa* factory and there's meat for days."

kubie

In Alberta, *kubie* is short for *kubasa* but is usually used when it is eaten on a bun like a *hot dog.*
"What's for lunch?"
"*Kubie* and *holubtsi.*"

kubie burger

In Alberta, *kubasa* pressed flat into a patty and eaten on a hamburger bun.
"What's for lunch?"
"*Kubie burgers* and perogies."

lacrosse

A sport stemming from the games of North American Aboriginals and introduced to Europeans by Jesuit missionaries who had been stationed in Canada. In its modern form, lacrosse is played by two opposing teams who fling a hard rubber ball at their teammates by throwing and catching it with small, loose nets attached to the ends of long sticks. The objective is to shoot the ball into the opposing team's goal, much like hockey. *Lacrosse* is Canada's official sport, so all you puck monkeys out there can suck it up.

La-La Land

A nickname for BC, possibly because of its perceived leisurely pace of life, or possibly because of its world-renowned marijuana. Overheard during rush hour in *Hogtown*:

"That's it. I'm quittin' my job and movin' to *La-La Land*."

language police

An informal and contemptuous term for "Office Québecoise de la Langue Française." The organization stems from one founded in 1961, when French Canadian culture and language were under a very real threat (especially in Montréal) from the predominant *anglo* culture. In its current form, the OQLF's most visible mission is to ensure that all of Québec's public signs conform to the law that states they must be predominantly in French. This stems from the perfectly reasonable expectation that French-speaking citizens of Québec should be able to be served in their native language. The OQLF responds to complaints from *francophones* who do not feel their needs are being met. However, in recent years, the *language police* have attracted negative attention for, among other things, notifying the owner of an Indian restaurant that he was breaking the law by having coasters advertising, "Double Diamond" beer. They also requested the clothing chain "Old Navy" to change its name to "La Vieille Rivière" (it didn't). However, to their credit, the *language police* do not appear to have acted when an irate woman complained that the parrot she wanted to buy from her local pet shop did not speak French (though one can easily imagine that they must have really gritted their "dents" over this one).

large day

In PEI, 1) A day in which much is accomplished. "Let's see, we whistled at some *dilseys*, found our lost *hand socks* and had *Frenchman's turkey* for supper. It was a *large day.* Time to *get to blanket harbour.*" 2) A fine bright day. (See also *not too bad of a day.*)

Last Best West

In olden-days Alberta, this was a flattering phrase to describe a new area of land, presumed to be the best available—ever.

"What do you think of our new riverside plot?"

"It's the *Last Best West.*"

Laura Secord (1775–1868)

A heroine of the War of 1812, famous for walking 30 kilometres on foot to warn British troops of an impending surprise attack by American forces. Acting on her information, the British foiled the attack during the battle of Beaver Dams. Her exploits are the subject of a *heritage moment.*

Laura Secord chocolates

A chocolate company founded in 1913 and named after *Laura Secord.* The founding of the chocolate company is **not** the subject of a *heritage moment.*

leave her lay where Jesus flang her

Friendly permission to not tidy something up.

"Shall I hang my coat up?"

"Nah, just *leave her lay where Jesus flang her.*"

lederhoser

One of that peculiar breed of Canadians who insist on wearing shorts at inappropriate times of year, such as when it is 30 degrees below zero.

(the) Legion

Short for *Royal Canadian Legion*. "Wanna go down to *the Legion* for a beer?"

Let the Eastern bastards freeze in the dark

A popular bumper sticker in Alberta during the time of the wildly unpopular *National Energy Program* (1980–85). This phrase is well remembered and presumably still used.

levee

A reception held on New Year's Day by public officials ranging in status from the governor general to local mayors.

"Goin' to the *levee* tomorrow?"

"Would I miss a chance to see the mayor get drunk and bob for apples?"

like an appetite with the skin pulled over her/him

In PEI, someone who is always hungry.

"When we were camping, my sister ate a few *digby chickens*, some *Frenchman's turkey* and a plate of *bush salmon* followed by *figgy duff* and *blueberry grunt*—and that was just for *mug up!*"

"She's *like an appetite with the skin pulled over her.*"

Lobster Lad

At one time, a nickname for someone from Newfoundland, although to modern ears it sounds more like the hapless sidekick of some Maritime superhero: "The Adventures of Cod Man and *Lobster Lad!*"

lobstick

A tall coniferous tree with all but the top branches lopped off to serve as a landmark for fellow travellers. "We must be on the right path—there's the *lobstick.*"

log drive

Cowboys have cattle drives; *lumberjacks* have *log drives;* that is, the mass transportation of logs to sawmills by floating them (the logs) down rivers. Overheard between a prairie cousin and a coastal cousin:

"I'm goin' on a cattle drive to Calgary."

"Well, I'm goin' on a *log drive* to the sawmill, so there."

log pirate

The practitioner of a singularly unambitious form of thievery that involved stealing (usually) single logs during *log drives.*

"Arr, we be *log pirates.*"

"Dude, there are so many things I could say to make fun of you that I don't even know where to start."

logger

1) Synonymous with *lumberjack.* 2) A person whose specialty is transporting and selling logs (as opposed to actually cutting the trees down).

logging bee

1) Historically, the mass clearing of land in preparation for a house raising or crop planting. 2) Other nations have quilting bees or even spelling bees, but only Canadians are so virile that we have *logging bees;* that is, contests of the lumberly arts (for example, tree climbing, log rolling, wood carving with chainsaws, and so on.)

lolly

In Atlantic Canada, floating slushy ice. "It's too early in the year for *copy*—there's no *ice pans* yet, just *lolly*." The word comes from British slang, "loblolly" for mush (often used to refer to porridge, stew or gruel). (See also *frazil, slurry*.)

loonie

1) A common way of referring to Canada's one-dollar coin, since one side shows a swimming loon. "Can you please give me a couple of *loonies* in my change? I have to do laundry today." 2) The Canadian dollar as referred to by economists, especially when comparing the *exchange rate* between the Canadian and American dollar. "The *loonie* dropped half a cent today to close at 86 cents American."

Lord Stanley's Mug

Slang for the *Stanley Cup*.

lorsh

In PEI, an exclamation or interjection, being

a combination of "Lord" and "gosh!" "*Lorsh*, what're you feeding this nephew of mine? He's growing like a weed!"

Lotus Land

A phrase allegedly coined by columnist Allan Fotheringham in reference to southern BC's balmy climate, but now also in wide use as a synonym for Vancouver specifically. "Come on out here to *Lotus Land* and relax for a few days."

loup-garou

To early French Canadian settlers, *voyageurs* and traders, a werewolf or wolf devil. "Loup" is French for "wolf," while "garou" stems from old French, "garoul," for "werewolf."

"*Tabernac!* What was that?"

"That's my mother-in-law."

"*Sacrement!* I thought it was the *loup-garou!*"

Lower Canada

A British colony on the banks of the St. Lawrence River in existence from 1791 to 1841. It encompassed the present-day regions of southern Québec and Labrador.

Lower Canada Rebellion

A series of conflicts between British forces and republican rebels occurring from 1837-38 and correlated to the *Upper Canada Rebellion*, which happened during the same period. As with the *Upper Canada Rebellion*, the rebel forces were

L

quashed, but the rebellion did lay the ground-work for future reforms in land distribution and self-government in Canada.

lumber jacket

A heavy felt jacket usually with a plaid-like check pattern of red and black **or** pale blue, red and black. As well as being worn by real *lumberjacks,* during the 1980s this was a popular item of garb for suburban youth, mainly male, who incorporated their *lumber jackets* into a layered look, sometimes wearing them over or under denim jackets, leather jackets and/or plaid shirts. Pants were invariably blue or black jeans—often very tight or full of holes. Rounding out this elegant ensemble was a pair of work boots with their untied laces loosely scrambled. Although these *hosers* didn't know it, they were actually laying the fashion foundations of the grunge movement. (See also *mackinaw.*)

lumberjack

A person whose profession it is to cut down and transport trees for commercial logging purposes. Since Canada is known worldwide for its thriving lumber industry, there seems to be a general perception that those of us not living in *igloos* are *lumberjacks. Lumberjacks* may be perceived as rough-hewn, jolly sorts, untainted by society, prejudice or personal hygiene, noble savages, as it were, rife with virility (even the female ones) and accustomed to quaint backwoods traditions such as stirring their tea with their thumbs, eating pancakes all the time and so forth. In short, the eccentric ideas that people may have about *lumberjacks* are too numerous and varied to contain in a short compilation such as this one, but needless to say, very few of them are likely accurate.

lumberjack breakfast

A name given to large breakfasts on the menus of roadside and family restaurants. Contents may vary, but a typical lumberjack breakfast can include eggs, bacon and/or sausage and/or ham, toast, pancakes and fruit. Whatever it may comprise, rest assured it will be big, very big. "We've got a *large day* in front of us, so I'll start with the *lumberjack breakfast*, please."

Mac-Blo

Short for "MacMillan Bloedel Ltd.," an international forest company that was a large-scale employer in BC until it was bought out in 1999 by Weyerhaeuser, a U.S. firm based in Seattle. "Got a job for the summer?" "Workin' for *Mac-Blo*."

mackinaw

1) Thick felt cloth made from wool, usually plaid. "I've got a nice bolt of *mackinaw* here that I could let you have for just one beaver pelt." 2) A *lumber jacket* made from such material. "It's cold outside, be sure to wear your *mackinaw*. 3) When preceded by "Holy," an exclamation of surprise, "Holy *Mackinaw!*"

maîtres chez nous (masters of our own house)

The re-election rallying cry of Québec premier Jean Lesage, presaging the *Quiet Revolution*.

make strange

Now equally well known as the more clinical

sounding "stranger anxiety," this term describes the normal state of babies who are shy or fussy around new people, usually starting when they are about five or six months old. This term is also heard in the UK and Jamaica, but not the U.S., so perhaps it is more frequent in English-speaking Commonwealth countries.

"He doesn't seem very happy to see me."

"Oh, he's just *making strange*."

make work

An initiative or structure designed to create employment. While they can do a great deal of good, *make work* projects, whether created by government agencies or private contractors, can also be fertile breeding ground for inefficiency and corruption.

"Why do they get our crew to come in and put the scaffolding up, and then a different crew to come in and take it down right away?"

"It's a *make work* project."

"This is no way to build an Olympic stadium."

Mange-toi du pain blanc

French for "Go and eat white bread!" that is more or less analogous to "Go suck a lemon!"

"Ton *cretons* ont goût de lard!" (Your *cretons* tastes like fat!)

"Mange-toi du pain blanc!"

mangeur de lard

French for "pork eater"; in this case a mildly

derogatory term referring to *voyageurs* who paddled only between Montréal and Grand Portage, thereby avoiding strenuous exertions during the winter months on more demanding routes. They ate vast quantities of salt pork and so earned their nickname.

mangia cake

1) (pron: MUNJ-a-cake) An insult meaning "cake eater," famously used by Italian Canadians in reference to non-Italian Canadians, especially those of typically British traits, manners and customs. "See how he lifts his little finger when he drinks his tea? What a *mangia cake!*" 2) (pron: MAWN-jee cake) The same phrase, co-opted and mispronounced by non-Italian Canadians, likely those of British descent, now applied to anyone of prim, proper or conservative tendencies regardless of ethnic background.
"It's after Labour Day and I'm wearing white!"
"Ooh, you're really livin' on the edge there, y'big *mangia cake*."

manitou

An Algonkian word for "spirit." For the Cree and Ojibwa, the chief deity is "Gitchi Manitou" or "great spirit."

MAPL

A rating system used to determine the *CanCon* quotient of music recordings. Noticed by sharp-eyed music buyers for years, the *MAPL* logo is a circle divided into quadrants, each containing one of the letters in *MAPL*. It is included on CD and music recording packaging in the hope that broadcasters, upon seeing it, will be more likely to play the recording because it will help them to meet their *CanCon* quotas. Generally, two or more of the quadrants must be black with a white letter indicating that these two requirements have been met and the recording therefore qualifies as *Can-Con*. The "M" means that the **m**usic was composed entirely by a Canadian. The "A" denotes that the **a**rtist performing the music or lyrics is a Canadian. "P" is for **p**roduction, meaning that the music is recorded wholly in Canada or performed and broadcast live, wholly in Canada. The "L" means that the **l**yrics are entirely written by a Canadian. There are various exceptions to the rules.

maple

The national arboreal emblem of Canada, which is a fancy way of saying the *maple* is our official tree. Aside from lending the shape of its leaf to our flag, the word "maple" is used in a variety of other contexts to suggest or reflect things Canadian (see *MAPL* above). It is a popular name for business, products and organizations.

maple leaf

1) The leaf of the maple tree. 2) Canada's national emblem. 3) The Canadian flag. "They were

proudly flying the *Maple Leaf*." 4) A metaphor for Canada itself, as in the song, "The *Maple Leaf* Forever" by Alexander Muir. 5) A popular name for businesses: *Maple Leaf* Daycare, *Maple Leaf* Meats, *Maple Leaf* Travel, and so forth.

Maple Leafs

Short for "Toronto *Maple Leafs*," *Hogtown*'s NHL franchise. Apparently at some point in the past, the puck-rattled brains of local hockey fans lost the ability to pluralize the word "leaf" and, instead of the "Toronto Maple Leaves," we wound up with the "Toronto Maple Leafs." This has unfortunately led to at least two consecutive generations of *hosers* who think that the plural of "leaf" is actually "leafs" and will peel off their *lumber jackets* and put up their *hand socks* when corrected.

maple sugar

Sugar made by boiling maple sap far beyond the point necessary to make *maple syrup*. Today, it is a popular treat and is also used to flavour many different sweets. At its most *kétaine, maple sugar* is also moulded into the shape of the *maple leaf* and sold as edible candy at souvenir shops, along with plastic *Mounties*, stuffed toy *beavers*, extruded vinyl *inukshuks* and *idiot sticks*.

maple syrup

Sweet, edible syrup extracted by evaporating maple sap, a process perfected by *First Nations* peoples long before the arrival of Europeans. The method then was filched and exploited for great monetary profit by Europeans. Still, no one will deny that it is delicious, with right-thinking folk regarding their waffles and pancakes as simply vehicles for *maple syrup*.

March break

A week-long break in March for public, secondary and high-school students. While it is also sometimes referred to as "spring break," this should not be confused with the bacchanalian orgy known as "spring break" in the U.S., during which lusty and libatious university students travel to warm climes for sex and alcohol. In Canada, the latter is known as *Reading Week*.

Maritimes

Short for "Maritime Provinces," technically meaning Nova Scotia, New Brunswick and PEI, but often also used to include Newfoundland (although collectively, Nova Scotia, New Brunswick, PEI and Newfoundland are properly referred to as *Atlantic Canada*.)

mat leave

Short for "maternity leave." Paid time off given to mothers of newborn children. While the term is the same in the U.S., the implications are considerably different. In Canada, mothers of newborns are entitled to a full year off at a minimum of 50 percent of their regular wages, paid for through *EI*. In the U.S., such packages are at the discretion of individual employers and the leave period is generally shorter.

matrimonial cake

In western Canada, a *date square*. This confusion of terms is sure to cause heart palpitations during cross-continental romances.

"What would you like for dessert?"

"I'm thinking a *date square*."

"You mean *matrimonial cake?*"

"Whoa! Whoa! Who said anything about getting married?"

maudit!

1) A *sacré* that more or less means "damn!"
2) When spelled with an extra "e" (Maudite) a popular brand of Belgian-style beer in Québec, its label featuring a canoeful of frantically paddling *voyageurs*, meant to represent the damned men of the *Chasse-galerie* legend.

mauzy

In Newfoundland, damp, foggy, misty or close weather. "It's a *mauzy* day. I can't see two feet in front of me."

May two-four weekend

A three-day weekend observed in celebration of Queen Victoria's May 24th birthday. While it is also known as the *Victoria Day weekend* and the 24th of May weekend, those who celebrate it by polishing off a *two-four* have renamed it thus. The holiday is always celebrated the last Monday on or before May 24th.

"We're going camping for the *May two-four weekend.*"

"Great. I'll get a couple of *forty-pounders* and a *two-four.*"

McKenzie Brothers

A pair of fictional siblings created and portrayed by *SCTV* cast members Rick Moranis (who plays Bob) and Dave Thomas (who plays Doug). The advent of the *McKenzie Brothers* marks one of the rare instances in which outrageous *CanCon* requirements actually worked. When *SCTV* took up residence at the *CBC*, an executive requested that the show come up with an extra two minutes of distinctly Canadian content. Rick Moranis and Dave Thomas thought this was ridiculous because, for the previous two years, the show had been written and performed mainly by Canadians, and taped and broadcast in Canada. To create two minutes of *CanCon* filler for each show, Moranis and Thomas got themselves a low-budget set consisting of two chairs in front of a map of Canada, a couple of parkas, a couple of *tuques* and some *stubby* beer bottles. They called their show the *Great White North*. With one camera operator standing behind a locked-off camera, they assumed their characters and proceeded to improvise on whatever stereotypical traits of Canadian life came to mind, saying *eh* at the end of every sentence, calling each other *hosers* and swilling beer out of *stubbies*. They taped an entire season's worth of two-minute fillers in one session and thought nothing more about it. Imagine their surprise when the *Great White North* segments became the most talked about section of *SCTV* broadcasts. Soon to follow was a hit-record album, a feature film and a crazed fad for all things McKenzie. Soon Canadians who had never said or even heard the word *eh* were interjecting it into everyday conversations, first humorously, then ironically and finally without even noticing they were doing it. Beer-swilling *hosers* everywhere had found their voices, and for a brief, shining moment, Canadians embraced an identity that had little to do with reality.

M

mechoui (pron: MAY-shwee)

In Québec, a meal of grilled lamb or mutton. Overheard in a Montréal restaurant frequented by *anglos:*

"*Mechoui?*"

"Gesundheit."

Medicare

In Canada, a program providing universal health care for all citizens, much to the combined envy and dismay of our friends *south of the border,* many of whom recognize its value but cannot help but feel that it is the thin end of a socialist agenda with the sinister intent of ensuring everyone can see a doctor without going bankrupt.

meilleur avant

French for "best before," familiar even to die-hard, but sometimes unwitting *anglos* since it appears frequently on food packaging.

"Hey, I bought some fancy French milk called *meilleur avant*."

"It's so romantic when you say that."

Mennonites

A sect of Anabaptists, practicing non-violence and, in many cases, abstaining from the use of technologies such as internal combustion engines and sometimes, electricity. There are Mennonite communities all across North America and scattered throughout Canada. Mennonite vendors are also found selling fresh meat, savoury baked goods and delicious preserves at regional and county fairs and flea markets.

merde

In Québec, "shit!" (usually pronounced *marde*).

"Le *dépanneur* est fermé." (The convenience store is closed.)

"*Marde!*"

mesachie

Chinook jargon for "evil" or "bad." "After you've been *drunk as a thousand dollars*, your breath is *mesachie*."

Métis (male/generic plural)/Métisse (female)

A person of mixed Aboriginal and European

(especially French) ancestry. The oppression and discrimination to which the *Métis* were once (and in some places still are) subjected is perhaps best indicated by the etymology of the word *métis*, which is Canadian French for "mongrel."

metric (system)

Canada's official system of measurement and only included here because Americans are still puzzled by it, which isn't surprising since, besides Myanmar and Liberia, the U.S. is the **only country in the world** not to have adopted the metric system.

"The *metric system?* Where I come from that's just another word for socialism."

"It's actually two words."

"See? It's one word in English and two words in *metric!*"

middle school

A school where only Grades 7 and 8 are taught (or Grades 7, 8 and 9 in provinces where high school starts at Grade 10). Called "junior high" in the U.S. and some parts of Canada, *middle school* is a transitional stage between public school and high school.

milk store

A convenience store selling milk and other sundries. In Québec, a *dépanneur*. "I'm going to the *milk store* for smokes."

minty

In *Winterpeg*, a term for "cool."
"*Portage and Main* is the windiest intersection in Canada."
"*Minty*, man, *minty*."

misery fiddle/whip

In logging parlance, a long, two-handled crosscut saw, operated by two people, one pulling from each end.
"Chainsaw's broken. Time to pull out the old *misery fiddle*."

missus

In Newfoundland, a traditional and affectionate term for the female in a relationship, with *skipper* being the equivalent for men. "I went over to see the *skipper* and his *missus*."

moccasins

Leather slippers traditionally worn by Aboriginal peoples, often trimmed with fur and decorated with beads. Nowadays, tourists often encounter them in souvenir shops along with *maple sugar*, plastic *inukshuks*, *idiot sticks*, plush toy *beavers* and *Mountie* figurines.

Mohawk Gas

(See *Husky station*.)

Molson muscle

A beer paunch (Molson being a prominent Canadian brewery).

"You've made a pretty good dent in that *two-four.*"

"I'm flexin' the old *Molson muscle.*"

Mon oncle Antoine

A seminal French Canadian film released in 1971, chronicling the 1947 Asbestos Strike and its subsequent impact on Québec culture.

"Hey, the video store has a *CanCon* section! Let's see, there's either *Goin' Down the Road* or *Mon oncle Antoine*. Excuse me, have you got anything else in the *CanCon* section?"

"Oh, sure, there's lots more, but people have rented them and that's what's left."

Monsieur Bonhomme

The mascot of *Carnaval* in Québec. *M. Bonhomme* is generally portrayed by a person in a snowman costume and is the very embodiment of jollity, wintry good will and, in fact, bonhomie.

Moosehead

The largest and oldest wholly Canadian-owned brewery, Molson having been absorbed into the Molson Coors Brewing Company, and Labatt fast disappearing into Anheuser-Busch InBev, formerly known as Interbrew. Also the name of the brewery's flagship brand of beer.

moosemilk

1) Home-distilled liquor. 2) A drink made from rum and milk.

"Care for some *moosemilk?*"
"I'd rather have *caribou.*"
"I don't have any *caribou.*"
"Well, I want *caribou.*"
"Look—*caribou, moosemilk*—they're both hootch named after ungulates. Give me a break here."

mossback

An old timer, especially one having unprogressive ideas.
"He thinks women having the vote is just a fad."
"What a *mossback.*"

mosser

In PEI, a person who harvests *Irish moss.* "My potato field is fallow so I think I'll become a *mosser.*"

moving day

In Québec, a tradition that sees most year-long leases expiring on June 30, making July 1 *moving day.* The tradition began during the days of the *seigneurial system* when landowners were forbidden from evicting tenants before the winter snows had melted. The resulting law set this date as May 1, but during the *Quiet Revolution* the provincial government changed the date to July 1 so that university students would not have to move during the school year. While the terminal dates of leases are no longer set by law, most landlords observe this tradition, especially in urban areas.

Mozusse!

A *sacré* that translates as "Moses!"

Mr. Dressup

A beloved *CBC* children's TV show that ran from 1967 to 1996. Played by Ernie Coombs, *Mr. Dressup* read stories, did crafts, drew pictures, painted paintings and presented other activities that celebrated and nurtured children's imaginations. At some point in the show, he would open up the "Tickle Trunk" and take out a few carefully selected costume pieces to show the kids at home how they too could dress up to be anything they wanted. In a small backyard tree house lived two puppets, *Casey and Finnegan*, who shared in *Mr. Dressup's* adventures. Broadcast every weekday morning on *CBC*, *Mr. Dressup* was a lasting and positive influence on at least two generations of Canadian children.

mucilage

1) Non-toxic adhesive paste usually supplied to schoolchildren in a translucent bell-shaped container with a red wedge-shaped nipple on the top for daubing it on to "cut and paste" projects. While it was normally referred to as "paste," the word *mucilage* was usually to be found moulded into the plastic bottle or the red rubber cap. "Billy, I know it's non-toxic, but you still shouldn't swallow your *mucilage*." 2) A nickname for chewing gum in western Canada of yore: "Billy, I know it's non-toxic, but you still shouldn't swallow your *mucilage*."

muffin

In 19th century Canada, an impertinent term applied to a woman who sat prettily beside her male companion on winter sleigh rides. Canada seems to have been slightly ahead of the curve in adopting chauvinistic terminology.

mug-up

A hot drink (typically tea) and a snack, especially as a break from hiking, travelling on foot or while camping. "Time for *mug-up*. Today it's *bare-legged* and *bannock*."

mukluk

1) A traditional knee-high *Inuit* boot, usually made from caribou hide or seal skin and often decorated with coloured beads and/or trimmed with fur. 2) Affectionate present-day slang for winter boots of modern manufacture. "Get your *mukluks* on. It's time to go *tobogganing*."

muktuk

An *Inuit* food usually consisting of the skin and blubber of one or more kinds of whales (especially narwhal). It can be eaten dried, cooked or raw. Not to be confused with *mukluk* (above).
"He's offering you *muktuk*."
"He wants me to eat his shoes?"

multicultural

Descriptive of a country or society that welcomes, celebrates and sustains many different cultures in addition to its own geographically specific or historically predominant ones. Canada touts itself as a *multicultural* society, though the jury is still out on how the experiment is going and by what standards to measure it.

muskellunge/muskie

A tough and aggressive species of *fish* that may grow up to 1.5 metres long and can tip the scales at 66 kilograms. Its name may be a combination of the Ojibwa words "maskinonge" (ugly fish) and "lunge" (lake trout). Or it may derive from the French expression "maggue allongée" for "long face."

"Would you date Pete?"

"Are you kidding me? He's got a face like a *muskie*."

Muskoka chair

An outdoor chair for use on docks, patios and lawns. Made from wooden slats about 10 to 12 centimetres wide, *Muskoka chairs* have fan-shaped backs and wide armrests that are handy for setting coffee mugs, wine glasses and beer bottles on. They are named for the southern Ontario *cottage country* region of the same name on the shores of Georgian Bay.

my son

In Newfoundland, a friendly form of address directed to males, regardless of age or relationship to the speaker. For instance, even little girls have been heard to call their younger brothers *my son*, just as younger men have been heard to address older men in this way. Along with *by*, it has become stereotypical shorthand to connote all things East Coast. "How far *after* bein' back *from away* are you, *my son?*"

N

Nanaimo bars

A sweet, delicious dessert that may or may not have been invented in Nanaimo, BC. Served cut into squares, *Nanaimo bars* have a foundation of cookie crumbs and chocolate, covered in a vanilla buttercream filling, the whole being surmounted by a layer of chocolate. The earliest documented use of the name *Nanaimo bars* comes from a 1956 United Church cookbook from Humboldt, Saskatchewan.

Nanook of the North

A 1922 silent, feature-length film by American filmmaker Robert J. Flaherty. Widely considered the first feature-length documentary, the film is inextricably associated with Canada, since it chronicles the struggle of an *Inuit* family in Canada's arctic, where it was shot. While Flaherty has been criticized by documentary purists for staging scenes instead of filming real events, the film broke new ground in both its subject matter and scope. However, some glaring and deliberate inaccuracies are worth noting. The protagonist's name was not, in fact, Nanook (Inuktitut for "polar bear"), but actually Allakariallak; the woman portraying his wife was not his wife; and although Flaherty insisted that Allakariallak hunt with a spear for certain scenes, modern firearms had long since been the *Inuit*'s preferred method of hunting.

National Energy Program (NEP)

A controversial program implemented by the federal government in 1980 under Prime Minister Pierre Trudeau. Intended primarily to keep oil prices low in the eastern provinces, the *NEP* capped domestic oil prices at values well below those of the global market, much to the chagrin of oil-rich provinces like Alberta, which was understandably miffed. The program resulted in the infamous Alberta bumper stickers that read, *"Let the Eastern bastards freeze in the dark."*

(Now, from Ottawa, the) National Research Council time signal. The beginning of the long dash following 10 seconds of silence indicates exactly...

The words preceding the *CBC*'s broadcast of the National Research Council time signal. Every day, since November 5, 1939, *CBC* listeners have heard a variant of this lead-in, making the time signal Canada's longest running and shortest radio programme. The beginning of the long dash usually indicates 1:00 PM local time ("1:30 in Newfoundland"). For many Canadians, these words produce a feeling of calm and a sense that all is well with the world.

Nelvana of the Northern Lights

A female Canadian superhero created by comic-book artist and writer, Adrian Dingle, in 1941. *Nelvana* lived among the *Inuit*, and her powers included travelling at the speed of light along the paths of aurora borealis and becoming invisible. She was the first Canadian female superhero and among the first in the world, debuting before Wonder Woman. It was in tribute to her that one of Canada's premiere animation companies, Nelvana Studios, is named.

new Canadian

1) A person newly emigrated to Canada. 2) When capitalized, a popular name for small businesses such as, *New Canadian* Auto Clinic, *New Canadian* Drain and Plumbing, *New Canadian* Lumber and Building, and so on.

Newfie

1) An informal nickname for someone from Newfoundland, once used disparagingly, but now generally affectionate. 2) Short form for the Newfoundland breed of dogs.

Newfie jokes

An embarrassing but undeniable fad in the 1970s and '80s that saw an entire spate of jokes denigrating the intelligence of Newfoundlanders; for instance, "Five Newfies drove their pickup truck into the bay. The two in the cab got out okay, but the three in the back nearly drowned because they couldn't get the tailgate down."

Newfoundland turkey

In PEI, a synonym for *Frenchman's turkey*.

NFB

(short for the National Film Board of Canada) An agency of the federal government that funds, produces and distributes documentaries, alternative dramas and animation reflective of Canadian culture and heritage.

NFB vignette

A series of short subject films produced by the NFB during the 1970s and 1980s that were broadcast in place of commercials during interstitial breaks in regular programming. Canadian TV audiences of a certain age will fondly remember being drawn into whimsical, wonderful worlds that faded to black all too quickly to be replaced by the tidy lines of type: "Produced by the National Film Board of Canada." Two of the most enduring and popular are "The Log Driver's Waltz" and "The Cat Came Back."

nine months of winter and three of poor skating/sledding

A popular way of describing the weather in Canada, with the division of months varying, depending on the climate in the part of Canada where the speaker lives; for example, in colder regions: *eleven months of winter and one of poor skating.*

no guff

An expression meaning "That's obvious!"
"Wow, you *Canucks* pay a lot of taxes!"
"No guff."

north of 60

1) The areas of Canada north of the 60th parallel, especially the Yukon, Northwest Territories and *Nunavut.* 2) When capitalized, the name of a *CBC* television drama that ran from 1992 to 1997 and focused on the struggle of a fictional Aboriginal community in the north.

North West Company (NWC)

A fur trading company active from 1779 to 1821, headquartered in Montréal but especially active in Canada's West. The *North West Company* was the *Hudson's Bay Company's* principal rival, and armed skirmishes were known to break out over trapping claims and other tensions. The *NWC* enjoyed great success, but as setbacks befell the fur trade in general, it was finally forced to merge with the *Hudson's Bay Company* in 1821 under pressure from a British government tired of the colonial hostilities between two British companies.

North West Mounted Police

The police force founded in 1873 that eventually

became the Royal Canadian Mounted Police (RCMP).

North West Rebellion

An unsuccessful 1885 uprising of *Métis,* Cree, Assiniboine and *First Nations* bands, led by Louis Riel and resulting in his execution by hanging. The *North West Rebellion* marked the final defeat of Aboriginal groups by European forces in Canada. (See also *Red River Uprising*.)

Not a fit day for a fence post (a day not fit for a fence post)

Descriptive of exceptionally cold or generally foul weather. "It's *mauzy* and *drashy—a day not fit for a fence post.*"

not charming likely

In PEI, not likely at all.
"You think I'll make a million as a *mosser*?"
"*Not charmin' likely.*"

not much upstairs but, oh, what a staircase

Descriptive of a person with ample physical charms but lacking in wit, intelligence, the ability to properly pronounce "nuclear" and so on.
"So what do you think of the best man?"
"*Not much upstairs but, oh, what a staircase!*"

not too bad

1) A characteristically Canadian reply when asked how things are going and generally meaning

N

"I can't complain." 2) An ironic, but genuine response to something exceptionally good and generally meaning "You've done well."

"I just won the lottery!"

"Not too bad!"

not too bad of a day

In PEI, 1) An exceptionally fine day. "The sun is shining and the birds are chirping—*not too bad of a day*." 2) An exceptionally cold or foul day.

"Here, take a look through the binoculars. Cousin Bob's got his tongue frozen to the *hydro* tower again."

"Not too bad of a day then."

Now wouldn't that jar your preserves!

An expression of surprise.

"Aunt Flo's *Nanaimo bars* won first prize at the church bake-off."

"Now wouldn't that jar your preserves!"

Nunavut

1) An Inuktitut word meaning "our land."

2) A Canadian arctic territory comprising areas of land once part of the Northwest Territories. It was created by act of Parliament in 1993.

O

O Canada

A patriotic song written in French to celebrate *Saint Jean Baptiste Day* in 1880, with an English version following in 1908. The original version featured music by composer Calixa Lavallée and lyrics by poet and judge Sir Adolphe-Basile Routhier. An English translation followed in 1906, and an all-new set of English lyrics in 1908, penned by Robert Stanley Weir, a lawyer. While it was sung for years as Canada's de facto national anthem, it was not officially accorded that status until 1980.

October Crisis

Events surrounding the October 1970 kidnapping (in Québec) of British Trade Commissioner James Cross and provincial Minister of Labour Pierre LaPorte by members of the Front de Libération de Québec (FLQ), a separatist group. Cross was eventually released, but LaPorte was murdered in captivity. Prime Minister Pierre Trudeau invoked the War Measures Act at the request of the premier of Québec and the mayor of Montréal. Before imposing martial law, when asked how far he would go to restore order, Trudeau famously replied, "Well, *just watch me*."

off-sale

In BC, Alberta and some northern territories, the sale of liquor, usually from hotels, to be consumed in a different location. This is different from all the other provinces, in which the purchase of liquor for personal use away from the point of purchase is restricted to traditional retail establishments. Locations offering *off-sales* have the advantage of being open for longer hours than most beer or liquor stores.

Ogopogo

A legendary, serpentine monster said to inhabit Lake Okanagan in BC, *Ogopogo* can be thought of as Canada's Loch Ness monster.
"Good heavens! Is that *Ogopogo?!*"
"Only if it's not a plesiosaur."

old home week

1) An informal expression for any festive time when members of a family or community return home for visiting and celebration. It is most often used as a simile when several friends, former co-workers or family members all unexpectedly see one another in quick succession: "First I ran into cousin Bob, then Uncle Pete and now you. It's like *old home week* around here."

(the) old woman's plucking her geese today

A folk saying that references a heavy snowfall of fat, wet flakes resembling white feathers floating down from the heavens. The identity of the afore-said old woman remains ambiguous.

on the bench

In hockey, a term to describe players, suited up and ready to play but sitting *on the bench*, waiting for ice time. As well as referring to players simply awaiting their turn, it may also describe players suspended from play for one or more games for a serious infraction.

"He's *on the bench* because he bludgeoned another player during a game."

"I wish they'd just let them play without all these stupid rules. Hockey is a violent sport, and you have to expect that people are going to get roughed up."

"Actually, they benched him for using a baseball bat and not a hockey stick."

"Oh, well, that explains it then."

On to Ottawa

An infamous 1935 labour movement, organized by the Communist Party of Canada. During the Great Depression, unemployed men were housed in federal "relief" camps all across the country. For 20 cents per day, they constructed roads and were used as cheap labour for other public works projects. Living conditions in the camps were notoriously bad, and their residents were not allowed to vote in federal elections. The Canadian Communist Party organized the men into the

Relief Camp Workers Union, and on June 3, 1945, hundreds of strikers boarded boxcars and headed east from Vancouver with the intent of taking their grievances to Ottawa. This was dubbed the *On to Ottawa* trek. When the trek reached Regina, a delegation of eight men was invited to Ottawa for talks with Prime Minister R.B. Bennet. After talks, the eight returned to Regina and began organizing the continuance of *On to Ottawa*. On the evening of July 1, 1935, the RCMP moved in to disperse the trekkers. In the subsequent riot, one RCMP officer was killed, and a trekker subsequently died from his injuries. The Bennet government's handling of the affair led to its downfall in the next election, and the *On to Ottawa* trek set the stage for the social and welfare reforms that were enacted following the Depression.

Only in Canada, you say? Pity.

The catchphrase of a popular series of television commercials for *Red Rose Tea* broadcast in the late 1970s and early 1980s. *Red Rose*'s blend of orange pekoe tea is available only in Canada, and the commercials featured characters with plummy English accents lamenting this fact with a whimsically mournful, *"Only in Canada, you say? Pity."*

ookpik

A doll resembling an owl, first produced by *Inuit* artisans, but now mass-produced as souvenirs.

"What are you going to call the souvenir shop

that you're opening?"
"*Ookpiks* 'n *Inukshuks*."

oolichan

Chinook jargon for a kind of small *fish (Thaleicthys pacificus)* known variously as candlefish, oil *fish* and salvation *fish*. Its oil (also called "grease") is useful and popular as an ingredient in sauces for foods. "That *oolichan* grease smells *mesachie*."

ooloo

An *Inuit* knife with a bone handle and a blade shaped like a slice of pie with the cutting surface on the curved edge, and the handle attached to the point. *Ooloos* were traditionally used by *Inuit* women for any number of domestic tasks.
"The *kabluna's* got his tongue stuck to your *snow machine* again."
"Pass me my *ooloo*."

open and shut day

A folksy way of describing the weather on a day that is sunny with cloudy periods. "It's an *open and shut day* today."

Orchard City

A large patch of apple orchards located in and around Kelowna in BC's interior. "If you're looking to become a *fruit rancher*, you should drive through *Orchard City* and check things out."

Order of Canada

Canada's highest civilian honour, having three grades—member, officer and companion.

OT

Short for "overtime," in reference to the extra period(s) of hockey played when the score is tied after the regular three periods of play.

our home and native land

A line from "*O Canada*," sometimes used as shorthand for Canada itself.

outport

1) In Newfoundland, any coastal settlement other than *St. John's*. "Compared to the *outports*, *St. John's* is very cosmopolitan." 2) In the *Maritimes*, any coastal fishing village. "I've finished writing my collection of short stories about the *Maritimes* and I'm calling it 'Tales of the *Outports*.'"

outporter

An inhabitant of an *outport*. "A boatload of *outporters* just tied up at the dock."

Outside

In parts of northern BC, Yukon and *Nunavut*, a term that refers to larger communities in more populous areas. In some ways it can be seen as roughly analogous to the Maritime phrase "*from away*."

"How'd he get his tongue stuck to his *snow machine* like that?"
"He's from *Outside*."
"Well, that explains it."

P

packsack

A knapsack or backpack. The term *packsack* is used sporadically all across Canada, but especially in northern parts of Ontario and Alberta. However, since most Canadians say "knapsack," hearing *packsack* is generally cause for comment: "Did you just call it a *packsack?*"

pamplemousse

French for "grapefruit." This is another French word widely known among *anglos* from its frequent appearance on juice labels.

"I can speak French!"

"No, you can't."

"Yes, I can."

"Okay, speak some French for me."

"Uhhh…okay…uh…*beurre d'arachides*…and—et *d'ananas*…and uh…*meilleur avant pamplemousse.*"

"Congratulations. You've just told me that peanut butter and pineapples are best before grapefruit."

"Well…they are!"

panzerotto

Now more frequently called "pizza pockets," *panzerottos* consist of pizza filling contained by a circle of dough folded in half to form a semicircle. They were, and probably still are, a popular food in high school cafeterias.

"The new exchange student said he wanted to have a really Canadian meal, so I'm getting him a *panzerotto*, some *ketchup-flavoured chips* and a *Jos. Louis*."

"Good. And then when he's *reconsidering lunch* you can teach him how to say *beulah*."

Pardon me

A well-mannered request for a speaker to repeat something he or she has said. While it is not an exclusively Canadian phrase, *Pardon me?* is often cited as an example of our supposed penchant for being unfailingly polite. It does, after all, sound much more pleasant than the gracelessly utilitarian "What?" It is perhaps the surprise of hearing people actually say *Pardon me?* rather than "What?" that leads non-Canadians to comment on its use.

ParticipACTION!

A federally funded program to promote healthy living and physical fitness. *PartcipACTION* initially ran from the early 1970s to 1991, when it was halted because of (what else) funding cuts. One of its earliest and most famous TV spots compared the fitness of a 30-year-old Canadian to that of a 60-year-old Swede. Eventually the campaign's call to action became, "Don't just think about it, do it!" This phrase was also the first line of a dreadful jingle that rhymed "water" with "oughta" and, most disturbingly, "weekend" with "fatiguin'." *ParticipACTION* was revived in 2005 and continues to the time of this writing.

PD Day

Short for "Professional Development Day," a day on which school classes are cancelled so that teachers can attend seminars, lectures and other events that constitute "professional development." Even very young children tend to know this term because it is synonymous with not having to go to school.

"It's a *PD day* tomorrow."

"Yesssssssss!"

peameal bacon

1) A lean cut of bacon of which the entire rasher is rolled (originally in peameal, but now usually) in cornmeal, so that when it is cut into slices, the outer edge still has a crisp coating of crumbs. It is also called *back bacon* and *Canadian bacon*.

pecker pole

In *lumberjack* parlance, a small tree, hardly worth logging. "I'm only cutting down this *pecker pole* because it's in our way."

(the) Peg

Short for Winnipeg. "*Portage and Main*, the so-called windiest intersection in Canada, is located in *the Peg*."

Peter Puck (a.k.a. The Irrepressible Imp of the Ice)

A vapidly grinning animated puck character invented in the 1970s to explain the rules and history of hockey. *Peter Puck* segments appeared in commercial breaks during *Hockey Night in Canada* and on some U.S. networks as well. The most gratifying thing about them is watching Peter get violently hit with hockey sticks, which he only faintly protests.

PetroCan

A publicly traded oil company, originally founded as a *Crown corporation* in 1975 under a minority government headed by Pierre Trudeau. Wildly unpopular in oil-rich Alberta (and really, what isn't), *PetroCan* was initially a tool of the federal government in its quest to redistribute the wealth generated by Alberta's oil industry. Understood to be a contraction of "petroleum" and "Canada," westerners interpreted it to mean "Pierre Elliott Trudeau Rips Off Canada."

Plains of Abraham

The site of an infamous battle between French and English forces on September 13, 1759. The English were victorious, and the battle's outcome effectively paved the way for the end of French rule in Canada. Many French Canadians are still upset about it.

plastic bread

In PEI, industrially baked white bread (also called *baker's fog*), correctly perceived to be insubstantial compared to the heartier home-baked variety. Overheard in a PEI diner:

"This sandwich is made from *plastic bread* and *processed cheese*."

"Great! Your meal consists entirely of edible petroleum products."

playoff beard

A long-standing tradition in which hockey players (and sometimes fans) grow beards for the duration of their playoff run, only shaving them off once their team has been eliminated or wins the *Stanley Cup*, although in the case of the Toronto *Maple Leafs* (or as some call the team, the "Maple Laughs"), only the former applies.

playoffs

In Canada, a time of national mass dementia that lasts from late spring to mid-summer and during which NHL teams battle it out for possession of the *Stanley Cup*. If there are regularly scheduled TV shows you like to watch, you can pretty much kiss them goodbye during the *playoffs*. It is also impossible to go to a bar for a quiet drink during the *playoffs*, since quiet watering holes tend to become populated with crazed, jersey-clad zombies with painted faces who scream and yell at the small glowing box that shows them graven images of their false idols.

please
A word, the unthinking use of which frequently distinguishes Canadian travellers from American tourists, especially in U.S. itself and other English-speaking countries.

plough (vs. plow)
Canadian spelling for the American "plow." Not noted for embracing silent consonants, our American cousins may pronounce the Canadian spelling as "ploff" when reading catalogues at agricultural fairs.

pogey/pogy
Employment Insurance or *EI* (formerly *Unemployment Insurance*). Many people incorrectly use *pogey* to describe welfare, which it is not. In reference to *EI*, however, it can be used as follows:
"I'm waitin' for *pogey* to come in." OR
"I'm on *pogey*."

pommes de terre
French for "potatoes," literally "apples of the earth," which is a generous description for these starchy root vegetables. *Pommes de terre* is a term well known to many Canadians who see it on food packaging.

P

poor man's fertilizer

In PEI, a late spring rainfall.

"Crops are lookin' dry."

"We can always hope for *poor man's fertilizer*."

pop (vs. soda)

Pop is how Canadians refer to the sweetened, flavoured, carbonated beverage that Americans call "soda." In Canada, "soda" is typically used when ordering a mixed drink, such as "Scotch and soda." In cases like this, it refers to "Club Soda," a colourless, flavourless fizzy drink mixer. Saying *pop* instead of "soda" is one of the most well-known differences between Canadian and American English, but this fact still doesn't serve to diminish the awkwardness.

"Have you got any soda?"

"Aha, see, I know that you're really asking me for a sweetened, flavoured, carbonated beverage, known as *pop* in Canada incidentally, and not the colourless, flavourless fizzy drink mix that Canadians typically call 'soda.'"

"Er...right...so have you got any?"

porch climber

1) In BC, cheap red wine available during the fledgling days of the province's wine industry. *Porch climber* came in gallon jugs with handles on the necks, and once it was drunk, so were those who drank it. Apparently its powers of inebriation were so potent that otherwise calm

and collected folk tried to shimmy up the porch posts, whence comes the name. "You brought *porch climber?* I'm throwing a dinner party, not an orgy." 2) Home-brewed liquor. "Look at this, I've got a nice bag of *porch climber.*"

portage (pron: por-TAWZH)

1) A verb to describe the act of carrying canoes and supplies (sometimes considerable distances) overland to get to the next navigable waterway. *Voyageurs* were infamous for *portaging*, and modern-day campers do it, too. In a sentence of *Franglais*, it might be used thus: "Well, mes amis, c'est time for us to *portage*." 2) A noun to describe an instance of *portaging*. "We did a *portage* over Heartbreak Mountain, around the Giant *Pysanka* and along Cripple Creek to Mosquito Slough."

Portage and Main

1) The so-called coldest and windiest intersection in Canada (despite the fact that Canadian inter-sections are not measured for these sorts of things), located in downtown Winnipeg. In this case, *Portage* is not pronounced "por-TAWZH," but rather, to rhyme with "porridge." When someone pronounces it "por-TAWZH," they are most likely Canadian since they clearly know the word, but not how to say the name of the street. People who pronounce it to rhyme with "por-ridge" are either from Winnipeg, simply know their Canadian intersections or are American.

P

Located at the former heart of Winnipeg's financial district, *Portage and Main* is referenced in many Canadian songs, including the Randy Bachman/ Neil Young offering, "Prairie Town." 2) A synonym for Winnipeg itself, but rarely used in this sense.

postal code
The six character, alphanumeric code that pinpoints a particular area for mail delivery in Canada. Equivalent in function, but different in form, to "zip codes" in the U.S., *postal codes* run thus: letter, number, letter, space, number, letter, number, whereas zip codes consist of either five or nine numbers. Correspondents may employ a variety of techniques to remember frequently used postal codes. For instance, to remember the *CBC*'s postal code of M5W 1E6, some use the mnemonic "**M**ake **5** **W**ieners, **I**'ll **E**at **6**" (even though it's properly a "1" and not an "I").

P

potlatch
1) A *Chinook jargon* verb for "to give." "I'll *potlatch* you this *chic chic*." 2) A *Chinook jargon* noun for what would today amount to a gift exchange. "We're having a *potlatch* on Saturday." 3) Until banned by the federal government in 1884, potlatches were a tradition among the coastal tribes of the west, who assembled to give one another extravagant gifts. The reason they were banned, however, was because tribal chiefs insisted on

destroying large quantities of valuable goods in order to demonstrate their wealth to each other. This, in turn, brought great hardship on their people. The ban was lifted in 1951, presumably when a less wasteful giving ethos prevailed.

pot-walloper

In PEI, someone who washes dishes frequently.
"Can't your mother just relax after supper?"
"Nah, she's a real *pot-walloper.*"

poutine (pron: poo-TEEN)

French fries, cheese (or cheese curds) smothered in gravy. In 1957, Fernand Lachance, the owner of a snack bar in Warwick, Québec, was asked by a customer to combine French fries and cheese curds in a bag. Lachance replied that it would make a "maudite poutine" (a hell of a mess) but agreed to do it anyway, and so history was made. The word "poutine" already existed to describe an Acadian pie or pudding, something that was a mish-mash (or "mess") of ingredients. It probably came from a French bastardization of the English word "pudding." At some point Lachance also added gravy to his new concoction, and so was born arguably one of Canada's best-known exports.

poverty pack

1) A six-pack of beer. 2) A 15-pack (or other small pack) of cigarettes.
"Need anything from the *dépanneur?*"

"Can you spot me a *poverty pack?*"

"Beer or smokes?"

"Both."

prairie oyster

1) A drink taken in the belief that it will ease the pain of a hangover, consisting of a raw egg suspended in vinegar or brandy. "I definitely shouldn't have finished that *forty-pounder* last night. Can you make me a *prairie oyster?*" 2) Bull testicles cooked and eaten as food. "When I asked you to make me a *prairie oyster* for my hangover, I didn't mean bull balls!"

prairie schooner

A covered wagon or cart used by settlers during the westward expansion in the 19th century. "What you call a *prairie schooner,* we call a *chic chic.*"

process(ed) cheese

A thinly sliced species of edible yellow plastic that comes wrapped in cellophane. It is called "American cheese" by Americans, who mistakenly think it is actual cheese, and "cheese food product" by those who recognize that it is more chemical than bio-culture.

"This American cheese tastes specially good. Do you make it different up here in Canada?"

"Well, normally we take the cellophane off **before** we eat it."

puck bunny

A politically incorrect but entirely accurate descriptor for a woman who doesn't really like hockey but does like hockey players and will hang around rinks in the hopes of bedding them.

puck chaser/pusher

Slang for "hockey player."

puckster

Slang for "hockey player."

pull pole

To take down one's tent during a camping trip. "Well, the weekend's nearly over. Time to *pull pole* and get on the road."

pump sucker

A teetotaller or water drinker.
"I've offered him every kind of drink I can think of—*caribou, moose milk, porch climber*, even a *Bloody Caesar*—and he won't have any of 'em."
"Well, that's 'cause he's a *pump sucker*."

P

purple gas

On the Prairies, gas sold with lowered taxes to farmers for use in farm machinery. It is dyed purple so that unscrupulous folk cannot sell it at a profit.

put the bow to the fiddle

In PEI, to have a party.

"I just won the lottery! Time to *put the bow to the fiddle.*"

"*Hoot and holler and wave your donut!*"

pysanka (pl: pysanky)

An Ukrainian Easter egg elaborately decorated with intricate designs and vivid colours applied by dyeing the shell, marking it in great detail with hot wax dripped from a stylus, then dyeing it another colour so that the areas covered by the wax retain their original colour, and so on.

"Is that an argyle Easter egg you've got there?"

"It's a *pysanka!*"

qiviut

An Inuktitut word meaning fine, soft wool from the belly of a muskox. For English speakers, it is difficult to see how saying the word "qiviut" could be nearly as satisfying as saying "fine, soft wool from the belly of a muskox."

"This is some *qiviut* I brought back from my trip."

"What is it?"

"I was hoping you'd ask. It's fine, soft wool from the belly of a muskox."

Québecois

1) A noun denoting a French-speaking person from Québec. "He's a *Québecois*" or "She's a *Québecoise*." 2) An adjective to describe Québec's French-speaking people or culture. "He's *Québecois*." (Note: When used as an adjective, the feminine form *Québecoise* is rarely, if ever, used.)

question period

Following the British parliamentary system, this is an allotment of time set aside for members of the House to question government ministers.

When Canadians watch the news on TV and see our venerable members of parliament respectfully questioning one another, it is always during *question period*. Tight camera shots make it look as though everyone is in attendance, but this is a deliberate illusion. The customary practice is to seat all present MPs close together so that the House seems to be packed.

Quiet Revolution

A fundamental realignment of secular, religious and political influences in Québec, generally seen as taking place between 1960 and 1966, during the premiership of Jean Lesage. The provincial government took over responsibility for health care and education, which up to that time had been overseen by the Catholic church. This marked a significant lessening of the church's influence in the day-to-day lives of Québecers. For the first time, unionization was allowed in the province's civil service. Electricity production and distribution was nationalized. Provincial politics became defined by separatist and federalist forces.

Raised chocolate/maple

Descriptive of icing on *doughnuts* and, as such, used as a synonym for the *doughnut* itself. For instance, a *raised chocolate* is a plain circular *doughnut* with chocolate icing coating one face. This is in contrast to a "chocolate doughnut" that describes a *doughnut* made from dough that is itself impregnated with chocolate flavouring agents and colouratives. With the maple variety, the distinction is somewhat different: *raised maple doughnuts* are identical to *raised chocolate* except for the flavour of the icing; however, the "raised" nomenclature is used here to distinguish them from "maple cream" *doughnuts*, which are like *jelly doughnuts*, but with maple cream at the centre instead of jelly.

"Can I get a *raised chocolate*, please?"

"You sure you wouldn't rather have a *bismarck?*"

"Don't even get me started."

ranchers

In logging camps and on fishing vessels, a derogatory term to describe newbies. Actual *ranchers* in the Prairies may say that this is yet another case of east and west ganging up on the centre, but it's really just jobism.

"Did he just try to catch the falling tree?"

"What a *rancher*."

OR

"Tell me he didn't just cut the net loose."

"What a *rancher*."

rangy

1) (noun) A fit due to excitement, nerves or exasperation. "Don't take a *rangy*." It probably comes from the logging camp pronunciation "rangatang" or "rangytang," used to describe a "brush ape"; that is, a logger dangerous to co-workers either through recklessness or incompetence. 2) (adjective) Being in a state of visible agitation: "He's completely *rangy*."

rappattack

In BC, a contraction for "rapid attack" or "rappel attack," referring to the daring crews who rappel out of helicopters directly into the danger zone in order to better fight the fire.

Reading Week

For Canadian university students, a week-long break during which there are no classes. *Reading Week* usually occurs in late February or early March, ostensibly to allow students to catch up on reading and study, but often as not, it is either used for low-key relaxation or Dionysian debauchery.

"What subjects are you catching up on during *Reading Week*?"
"Are you high?"

reconsider lunch
To vomit. "Fred had a bit too much to drink last night and now he's *reconsidering lunch*."

Red River Cereal
A brand name of hot cereal (porridge) consisting of cracked wheat, rye and flax seeds. It is named after Manitoba's Red River of *Red River Rebellion* fame.

Red River Resistance (a.k.a. Red River Rebellion)
The name given to the formation of a provisional government formed by *Métis* leader Louis Riel in 1869 to govern what shortly became the province of Manitoba. The provisional government executed a resistor named Thomas Scott, and Riel went into exile (in Minnesota and then Montana) until 1889, when he returned to lead the *North West Rebellion*. When Manitoba entered confederation, many conditions of the government Riel had founded were met by Canada.

R

Red Rose tea
A brand of tea established by Thomas Estabrook in 1894 in St. John, New Brunswick. Most teas at that time were a blend of Japanese and Chinese strains, but by using leaves from India and Sri

Lanka (then known as Ceylon), Estabrook's Orange Pekoe blend achieved a new and pleasing flavour (supposedly by using only the top two leaves on each sprig). While *Red Rose* is available in the U.S., it is a different blend of leaves. The unique taste of the Canadian blend led to the infamous TV commercials of the late 1970s and early 1980s whose catchphrase was *"Only in Canada, you say? Pity."* *Red Rose* is also famous for including prize cards with scenes from nature and the animal kingdom as well as tiny ceramic figurines showing characters from nursery rhymes.

reeve

In Ontario and parts of western Canada, a *reeve* is an elected official who serves more or less as the mayor of a small township or community such as a hamlet.

referendum

A vote by any electorate on a specific question. In Canada, the question is always, "Should Québec separate/be recognized as a distinct society?" or some variation on this. Stockwell Day, leader of the now-defunct Alliance Party, once ran on a platform that if three percent of Canadians signed a petition requesting a referendum, then one would be held. Comedian Rick Mercer promptly got far more than three percent of Canadians to sign an online petition requesting that Stockwell Day change his first name to "Doris."

rejig

To rethink, retool, reconfigure or reorganize. "We've *rejigged* the set-up here so that you go past the cream and sugar **after** you've gotten your coffee."

reno

1) Short for the verb to "renovate." "We're going to *reno* the basement." 2) Short for the noun "renovation." "We did a *reno* in the basement."

res

Short for "residence" as in a college or university residence. "There's this guy in my *res* who's a total *lederhoser*."

return ticket

A plane, train, bus or boat ticket good for both the outward and the return legs of a journey. It is included here because it is commonly referred to in the U.S. as a "round trip ticket."

RevCan

Short for "Revenue Canada," the dreaded government agency that collects taxes.
"*RevCan's* on the phone for you."
"Tell them I've *gone to the sand hills*."

rez

Short for "reservation," a parcel of land granted by the federal government for administration and inhabitation by an Aboriginal *band*. "I live on the *rez*."

R

Rhinoceros Party

A satirical political party, much missed and sorely needed. Started in 1963 by Jacques Ferron, the party was initially created to run against Pierre Trudeau for his Montréal seat. Running on a platform described as two-feet tall and made of wood, the Rhino Party's one consistent campaign promise was to not keep any of its campaign promises. Although it never actually won a seat, legitimate political parties were often embarrassed by its strong showing. In 1993, it was struck from the rolls of official political parties because it could not field candidates in 50 ridings at a cost of $1000 per candidate, as new legislation required. Some of the Rhino Party's campaign promises included repealing the law of gravity; paving Manitoba to create the world's largest parking lot; providing higher education by building taller schools; putting the national debt on VISA; painting the international boundary on the surface of the ocean so that Canadian *fish* would know where they were at all times; and making the *TransCanada Highway* one-way only. Once, after a prolonged absence from the political scene, the Rhinoceros Party returned with the comforting announcement that their time away had all been a dream.

rhyme off

To state a list of items off the top of your head or from memory. "It's amazing. She *rhymed off* all of the *Rhinoceros Party*'s campaign promises just like that."

riding the pine

Descriptive of a hockey player who spends a lot of time *on the bench*. "It's been ages since he got any ice time. He's been *riding the pine* for three games in a row."

road apples

A slang term for horse or cow manure that has settled and frozen into a disc shape. Appropriately enough, *road apples* were often used as pucks for games of *road hockey*.

road hockey

An informal game of hockey played in the street by active children, wayward youth and adults with nothing better to do. In its modern form, it is usually played with regular hockey sticks, but with a tennis ball instead of a puck. If real nets are not available, the goals can be represented by rocks, sticks or even clothing items strategically placed. In the olden days, players used *road apples* as pucks. (See also *Car!* and *Game On!*)

Robertson screw

Screws with a square notch in the head, used primarily in Canada and sporadically in other countries where they may be called "square head" or "square drive" screws. Canadian inventor P.L. Robertson invented them in 1908, and he

R

ultimately had to buy back the rights to his own invention from unscrupulous screw manufacturers. Henry Ford is reputed to have wanted to use *Robertson screws* in his automobile factories, but Robertson refused to license them to him since there was no guarantee they would actually be used.

ROC

Rest of Canada, when speaking from inside, or in reference to Québec (grave consequences may ensue if this contraction is confused with "ROC" when it is used to mean "Republic of China").

(The) Rock

Slang for Newfoundland, though many Americans may think the speaker is referring to pro wrestler-turned-actor Dwayne "The Rock" Johnson (who is American).
"Are you going home to Canada for Christmas?"
"Yup. Headin' back to *The Rock*."
"I didn't know The Rock was Canadian!"

rock doctor

Slang for "geologist." "She's *goin' down the road* to become a *rock doctor*."

(the) Rockies

Short for "Rocky Mountains."
"*The Rockies* date from the Precambrian and Cretaceous periods with a geology of igneous, metamorphic and sedimentary rock."
"Only a *rock doctor* could *rhyme off* all that."

Roll Up the Rim to Win

A seasonal promotion by *Tim Hortons*, in which customers unroll the tightly curled paper rim of their disposable coffee cups in search of printed words informing them they have won prizes. It has entered the general lexicon and is an immediately identifiable phrase to most Canadians.

"It's *Roll Up the Rim to Win* time."

"All I ever win is a free muffin."

(la) rondelle ne roule pas pour lui

In Québec, a saying that translates as "The puck isn't going his way" or "The puck is not rolling for him."

"He went to the *caf* for some *poutine* and spilt it all over his *mukluks*."

"La rondelle ne roule pas pour lui."

roof (vs. "ruf")

While not technically a different word, the strange way that some Americans pronounce the word "roof" justifies its inclusion here. Canadians pronounce the double "o" so that it sounds like the word "you," whereas some Americans pronounce it like "push," making them sound as though they're poorly imitating a small dog.

room

In Newfoundland, a waterfront tract of land where fishery operations are conducted. This is one of those terminologies sure to confuse those not in the know.

R

"Wanna come see my *room?*"
"Uh...I'm really just here for the fishing."

rotten ice
Ice that has melted to a point that it is no longer entirely solid, though it may appear to be solid on the top.
"Would you call that *frazil?*"
"No."
"*Lolly* then?"
"Nope, it's *rotten ice.*"

Royal Canadian Legion (a.k.a. the Legion)
A non-profit veteran's organization founded in 1925 for those who have served in the armed forces or various police forces—and their direct relatives. In smaller communities (and some larger ones), *the Legion* may be a social hub, because it usually offers economically priced alcoholic beverages in an informal, no-nonsense atmosphere. *Legion* halls may also serve as venues for community events, being licensed to serve alcohol and usually available to rent for an evening at reasonable cost. Sadly, in some larger cities, *the Legion* has begun to sell off its halls to real estate developers since the land they are situated on is worth more money than the income they bring in. This means that less and less is heard the friendly query, "I'm goin' down to *the Legion* for a *brewski.* Wanna come?"

rubbers
1) Galoshes or rubber boots. 2) Erasers. 3) Condoms. It's fairly easy to see how extreme discomfiture might result if any of these uses were to be confused one with the other, and so in the interests of modesty, this writer declines further comment.

rubby
One whom some call a "bum," others call a *rubby*. With "bum" being common both north and *south of the border*, it's only in Canada that people will say *rubby* to describe one of those poor unfortunates found begging on street corners and living under bridges. The root of this term comes from a practice common to many of them of drinking **rubb**ing alcohol, aftershave or even mouthwash, often mixed with rum, wine or some other more palatable alcoholic beverage. However, in recent years, the term *rubby* has come to be applied to any homeless, transient or vagrant person, especially men.

"Would you call homeless person a 'bum' or a *rubby?*"

"I live in Victoria, so I don't know what you're talking about."

runners/running shoes
Canadians say *running shoes* whereas Americans are more likely to say "sneakers" (though many Canadians say this too), and of course the English are shod in "trainers." In this case, Canadians and

Americans will understand each other perfectly, but English interlopers will be left scrambling for comprehension.

"Hey, pardner, my cowboy boots have bit the dust. Where can I buy a good pair of sneakers?"

"That store over there sells lots of different kinds of *running shoes.*"

"Thanks."

"Tally ho, chaps! I mean to say, don't you know, by Jove, wot! Where can I purchase a pair of trainers?"

"Who's the limey and what's he saying?"

"No idea, Tex. Good luck with your shoe shopping."

S

sacré

A French Canadian curse referencing Roman Catholicism, its liturgy and rituals; for instance, *Sacrébleu!* and *Sacrement!* Recorded as early as 1830, they coincided with increased resentment towards the dominance of the Roman Catholic church and its influence on the everyday lives of Québecers.

Sacrébleu!

A *sacré* often depicted as being uttered by either French or French Canadian characters. While it is a curse in European French, it has become equally associated (rightly or wrongly) with French Canada. Its meaning stems from some sort of blasphemous utterance, but it is unclear exactly what. It may mean, literally, "sacred blue," blue being a colour sometimes associated with the Virgin Mary. Or, in Canada especially, it **may** connote the sentiment, "I curse by God."

Sacrement!

A *sacré* that references the "sacrement" of the Catholic church. It is more or less equivalent to the English "Goddamn it!"

Saint Jean Baptiste Day

The former name (but still commonly used) for the *Fête nationale*, taking place on June 24. Saint Jean Baptiste is the patron saint of French Canadians, and his feast is celebrated on this day.

Sally Ann

1) Short for "Salvation Army," the Christian charitable group and church whose goal it is to bring "salvation" to the poor. In the U.S. it is called the "Sally Army," and in Australia, the "Salvos" or "Starvation Army." 2) Either *Sally Ann* or "Salvation Army" may be used to refer to retail outlets, run by this group, that sell and take donations of second-hand goods.

"Where are you going with that bag of old clothes?"

"Gonna donate 'em to the *Sally Ann*."

OR

"Where did you get that bag of old clothes?"

"Bought 'em at the *Sally Ann*."

salt chuck

Chinook jargon for "salt water" and so "the ocean."

"Look at that *salt chuck*, all full of *oolichan*."

sashay

1) A gliding step used in both ballet and square dancing, and as such, a derogatory term to describe a mincing or effeminate gait; in short, walking with a lisp. Overheard at a ballet recital: "Even when he's not on stage anymore, he still

sort of *sashays* around." 2) A jovial substitute for "walk" in even the most virile of environments. "Put down your axe, and *sashay* on over here. I need help hitching these *pecker poles* to the *come-along*."

Saskabush

The city of Saskatoon.
"Whatcha doin' for the weekend?"
"Goin' to *Saskabush*."
"Sounds like a *wild and woolly* time."

Sasquatch

A large, hairy hominid of the crypto-zoological variety. Known also as "Bigfoot," the *Sasquatch*'s existence has yet to be proven, though many of us remain hopeful, if not exactly expectant. It is said to be up to three-metres tall with a long, lumbering stride.
"Was that a *Sasquatch* that just crossed in front of the car?"
"No, that was my cousin Pete *sashaying* across the road. He hasn't shaved yet today."

sawdust nobility

Affluent folk who have profited from ownership or involvement in logging, lumber and other woody enterprises. In some ways, comparable to the *fishocracy*. "Didja hear the one about the daughter of the *fishocracy* who married a son of the *sawdust nobility?* When their kids go fishin', they call 'timber'!"

S

Scarberia

A nickname for the borough of Scarborough, Ontario, that compares its desolate expanses of industrial mall frontage to the vast, untamed Siberian steppes.

Scarlem

A nickname for the borough of Scarborough, Ontario, that compares its high population of African-Canadians to the demographic make up of Harlem, New York.

scoff

In Atlantic Canada, an impromptu or hurried meal prepared for a party or on a boat at sea. It is called a *scoff* because, formerly, the ingredients were stolen or sneaked either from ship's stores, a household's larder or neighbouring farms. For the participants, *scoffs* meant good times with friends; for the people who were involuntarily providing the fare, they were a source of frustration, especially around Christmas when they were quite frequent. Nowadays, the practice of stealing the food has, for the most part, gone by the wayside, but the word prevails. "We've got guests comin'. Time to get a *scoff* ready."

screech

A potent blend of overproof rum made in and associated with Newfoundland, often also called "Newfie screech." Originally made with Demerara rum from the West Indies, *screech* now uses

Jamaican rum. Its name presumably comes from the gasp, gulp or "screech" emitted by persons first swallowing this fiery beverage. Although the term became widespread during the 1940s and '50s (allegedly because of an American GI who tasted it for the first time), the idea of associating screeching with strong rum is much older, with an appearance in print as early as 1904: "The great unwashed, if he's not squashed / Where rotten rum does flow, boys / 'Tis he will *screech* upon the beach."

screech in

An informal ceremony after which visitors *come from away* are considered to be honorary New-foundlanders. The first step is to kiss an actual fish on the mouth, preferably a *cod*, but apparently any other *fish* will do (the incidence of native-born Newfoundlanders who have actually done this is very low). The second step is to say the words, "Long may your big jib draw." And the third step is to down a shot of *screech*. There are, of course, variations, depending on which bar or fine drinking establishment one opts to patronize. Some may pose the question, "Is ye an honorary Newfoundlander?" The required response in this case is, "Indeed I is, me old trout, long may your big jib draw." After successfully completing this ceremony, visitors to *The Rock* are then considered honorary Newfoundlanders with all attendant rights and privileges, whatever those may be (probably buying a round for everyone at the bar).

scrimshanking

In PEI, a rarely heard (but no less excellent for it) expression for living in poverty.

"Did Walter just break his cigarette in two?"

"Sure, he's saving half for later—he's *scrimshanking* it these days."

scrod

In Newfoundland, a *cod* (or codling) smaller than usual and so less likely to be sold commercially. As such they are perfect "take-home" catch for fishermen and are frequently used as a household food.

"I can offer you a cup of *bare-legged* tea and some salted *scrod*."

"It's how long *after* your last job?"

scrum

The impromptu surrounding and interrogation of a politician by a crowd of usually jostling reporters. The expression comes from the sport of rugby in which all a team's forwards link elbows, put their heads down and clash with the like-linked members of the opposing team.

"Stephen Harper doesn't do *scrums*."

"What **does** he do exactly?"

scruncheons/scrunchions

1) Bits of animal fat or *fish* liver with the oil

rendered out. Depending on the animal they come from, *scruncheons* can be used either in the preparation of food or as fuel for fires. "Look, if the *scruncheons* don't taste good, we can always throw them on the fire." 2) Cubes of fatback pork, fried and served as a garnish especially over *fish* and *brewis*. In either case, a simile such as "crunchy meat curds" is not entirely inappropriate.

SCTV

A popular television comedy program that ran on various networks and in one form or another from 1976 to 1984. Named after the famous Second City improv troupe (from whence came most of the cast), *SCTV* formed the call letters for a small television station in the fictional town of Melonville. Each week audiences were treated to not only the programs and commercials it was supposedly broadcasting but also the station's behind-the-scenes carryings on. It launched the careers of regular cast members John Candy, Eugene Levy, Andrea Martin, Rick Moranis, Catherine O'Hara and Dave Thomas—all of whom wrote and contributed scripts. Among many other worthy infamies, *SCTV* spawned the *McKenzie Brothers*.

se pèter les bretelles

In Québec, figuratively to burst with pride; literally, to fart off one's suspenders.

sea-flea

A tiny one-man speedboat, usually having a hull shaped like an oval saucer and driven by an over-sized outboard motor. With their loud, grating and far-carrying sound, *sea-fleas* were the bane of *cottage country* from the late 1950s to the mid-1970s. In function (carrying dimwits in circles at high speeds with much noise) they are the fore-runners of today's seadoos.

"Is that a chainsaw I hear?"

"Nope."

"Someone using a router?"

"Nope."

"Okay, fine—it's a buzz bomb then, and the Germans are attacking."

"Nope—it's a *sea-flea*."

Sedna

The supreme being of the *Inuit*, female. *Sedna* oversees the seals and other sea animals. Traditionally, hunters would thank her if they had a good catch.

seigneurial system

In Québec, a feudal system of land tenancy established by France in 1627. The *seigneurial system* was characterized by division of land into long, narrow plots with one end close to the nearest river and the rest running back perpendicular to the shoreline. All of the land was owned by the King of France, who assigned supervisory authority to a "Seigneur"—often a noble or prominent military officer. The Seigneur then subdivided his long, thin lot among several tenants (or *habitants*), who cleared and farmed the land. Many of the *habitants* divided their plots of land within the seigneury among their children. With many of the *habitants'* children then subdividing their plot among their own children, it meant that farms became smaller and smaller as generations went by. Some seigneuries were managed by women, supervising the plots after their husbands' deaths, until their children came of age to assume tenancy. The *seigneurial system* was kept in place after the conquest of New France by Britain during the Seven Years' War. It was not abolished until 1854. For many Canadians of a certain age, the approximate meaning of the *seigneurial system* and *coureur du bois* may be all that they retain of their *middle school* Canadian history lessons.

Senior Kindergarten

Kindergarten for children aged five to six. Overheard in a Canadian schoolyard: "That's Dougie. He's in *Senior Kindergarten*. He can tie his own shoelaces. He's old!" (See also *JK*.)

serviette

A napkin (which Americans are more likely to say) for use when eating, especially a disposable paper one. "Look, it's *mug-up*. You don't need to fold the *serviettes* into little swans."

S

shag

A *stag and doe* party, from a contraction of the words "shower" and "stag." Sure to cause confusion with visiting Brits, for whom "shag" means "to have sex with."

"Are you coming to our *shag* party?"

"A *shag* party? I mean to say, don't you know, by Jove, wot!"

shake hands with the bishop/shake the dew off of my lily

Euphemisms for urinating; in short, to pee.

"Where were you?"

"I was *shaking hands with the bishop*."

"*Shaking the dew off your lily?*"

"Indeed, I was *draining the main vein*."

shaker

In the *Maritimes*, a person in a lobster factory whose job it is to shake the meat out of lobster claws. After this, the claws are passed to the *knuckle picker*.

"I worked as a *shaker* for years, but I had to quit because of repetitive strain injury."

"Well, I worked as a *knuckle picker*, and I quit 'cause of all the cats following me home."

shakin' stick

In the tobacco industry, a position long since replaced by automation, in which a labourer took down a heavy rack of kiln-dried tobacco and shook it to make all of the toasted tobacco leaves

288

fall off. (See also *hangin' kill*.)

"I told my grandmother that I had a job for the summer *shakin' stick*, and she wanted to wash my mouth out with soap."

"Did she?"

"Well, nearly. She's 105, but she's strong."

sharp as a beach ball

This describes someone who is, not to put too fine a point on it, dumb as a stump, stupid as a post, thick as a brick wall, and so forth.

"Have you met Julie's new boyfriend?"

"He wears his sunglasses at night."

"He says it's so he can look cool when he bumps into things."

"*Sharp as a beachball*, that one."

s/he was pure as the driven snow, but s/he drifted

Descriptive of a person once of upstanding moral rectitude (or as some might say, tight-assed) but who now enjoys vice more than virtue.

"She used to be my Sunday school teacher and then I saw her smokin' and drinkin' and dancin' down at *the Legion*.

"Guess *she was pure as the driven snow, but she drifted*."

s/he's a temper in search of a tantrum

Descriptive of someone with a short fuse, possibly with a predilection for infantile confrontation.

"That prime minister of ours is a *temper in search of*

a tantrum."

"Yeah, he's what we call a sore winner."

shebang

1) A hut, shed or other rough structure that serves as a drinking establishment, especially in a rural or backwoods location. "I just traded forty beaver pelts to *the Bay.* Let's find a *shebang* and get *drunk as a thousand dollars."* Possibly, it may derive from the Irish Gaelic "shebeen," which also means a small or low drinking establishment. 2) As part of the expression, "the whole *shebang,"* it means the whole kit and kaboodle, the whole nine yards, the total package, etc.

"So you're telling me that the *kabluna* got drunk and lost my sled, my dogs and my fishing tackle?"

"Yup, the whole *shebang."*

shinplaster

1) Historical slang for a bank note worth 25 cents, because of its resemblance to a square piece of paper soaked in vinegar and used as a bandage on the shin. 2) In modern parlance, a worthless document or paper whose only value is as a shinplaster.

"What's this?"

"Canadian Tire money."

"Okay, so what are these *shinplasters* good for?"

shirt waist

In western Canada of yore, a woman's blouse,

usually made from different material than the skirt that went with it. These items are to be found throughout the mail-order catalogues of the day. "Ladies' *shirt waists*, reasonably priced from $1.25."

shit disturber

1) A person who revels in causing trouble. "He put a tack on the teacher's chair, dropped a water balloon on the custodian and poured flour in everyone's mittens. He's a real *shit disturber*."
2) Someone seen as positively pro-active but pushy.

shithawk

In urban centres, a pigeon (don't be fooled by elitists and bird-huggers who call them "rock doves").
"Get that *shithawk* away from my car."
"It's a rock dove."
"Okay, then you can clean its rock droppings off my hood."

shivaree

A noisy, boisterous celebration on the occasion of a wedding. Stemming from the old French word "charivari," the custom spread to Acadian regions of North America with the word now rendered *shivaree*. While everyone agrees noise must be involved, preferably the banging of pots and pans and possibly the firing of guns into the air, some practitioners initiate the *shivaree* as a friendly send-off when the bride and groom drive away after the wedding. Others wait until the evening, sneak up on the couple's house and only then commence banging and clattering to embarrass the newlyweds on their wedding night.

shore mosser

A person who gathers *Irish moss* from the shore.
"I used to have bigger dreams in life than bein' a *shore mosser*."
"Like what?"
"Like movin' to *The Rock* and bein' a *knuckle picker*, maybe move up to *shaker*."

short taken

To be in a state of really, urgently, desperately needing to *go to the washroom*, and so to take abrupt steps in order to achieve this goal.
"I know these family reunions are boring, but even so, Aunt Flo seemed to make an unduly hasty exit."
"Well, she was *short taken*, you know."

Shreddies

The brand name of a breakfast cereal sold in Canada, the UK, Australia and Ireland, but unknown in the U.S. It consists of small, flat squares of shredded wheat with the strands woven together in an overlapping pattern. Two advertising campaigns from Canada are worth noting: first, the ubiquitous "Good, good, whole wheat Shreddies" jingle, instantly recognizable to millions of Canadians;

and second, the campaign that reinvigorated the brand by hearkening the arrival of "Diamond Shreddies"; that is, a regular square *Shreddie* shown on the box and TV ads positioned such that one corner points downwards to resemble a diamond. "The last cereal to have a decent prize in the box in this country was *Shreddies*."

sidehill gouger

In BC, a mythical four-legged beast, whose right legs are shorter than its left legs, thereby enabling it to stand upright on steeply sloping mountain-sides. Although it has never been seen, its tracks are often observed as spiral gouges encircling a mountain.

"I think I hear a *sidehill gouger* on the other side of the mountain."

"Maybe it's with Bigfoot and *Ogopogo* and *Sisiutl*."

sign law

An informal term for the Québec laws stating that French must be the predominant language on public signage. For a fuller explanation, see *language police*.

silver thaw

In BC and the *Maritimes*, freezing rain that covers exposed surfaces in a thin layer of glittering ice. While *silver thaws* are undoubtedly dangerous for both drivers and pedestrians, they are also very beautiful, lending an enchanted air to a winter's

S

293

day. "Look, there's been a *silver thaw*—everything's sparkling!"

SIN

Short for "Social Insurance Number." This phrase is almost always spoken as the word "sin," leading some to redundantly ask "What's your *SIN* number?" meaning literally "What's your Social Insurance Number Number?" A *SIN* is the nine-digit identifier that all Canadians must have to legally work, be eligible for health care, collect Canada Pension Plan benefits and, of course, pay taxes. It is roughly equivalent to the American Social Security Number, but difference in terminology can be confusing.

"I've just moved here from the U.S. and I'm looking for work."

"Do you have a *SIN?*"

"Well, if anything, it's pride—you see, I know a lot about foreign customs and such and I'm proud of that."

Sisiutl

A legendary shape-shifting sea serpent of West Coast Aboriginal peoples. *Sisiutl* has two heads and can take the form of both living creatures and inanimate objects. An angry look from him can turn people to stone. Sometimes he is painted on the fronts of houses for protection. "Let's ask for directions here—they've got *Sisiutl* over the door."

sked

Slang for "schedule," assuming that it is pronounced (properly) with a "sk" sound instead of a "sh."

"What's your *sked* this *aft*?"

"Ohmigod, I'm supposed to have English, but, like, Ohmigod, the teacher is so mean! She won't even let you swallow your gum."

"Ohmigod! What is her problem? I love swallowing my gum."

skidder

In logging lingo of yesteryear, a *skidder* was a logger who hauled logs with a team of horses or maintained the skid road the horses trod. These days it refers to large, industrial moving vehicles with giant tires and huge pincers on the front for picking up logs. In all but name, *skidders* are sophisticated bulldozers for the logging industry.

Ski-doo/skidoo

1) When capitalized and hyphenated, a famous brand of snowmobile. 2) When not capitalized or hyphenated, any snowmobile regardless of make, in much the same way that the brand name Kleenex is used in reference to any disposable tissue.

"What kind of the *skidoo* do you have, Bud?"

"It's a *Ski-doo*, Lou."

"I know it's a *skidoo*. What **kind** of *skidoo* is it?"

"It's a *Ski-doo skidoo*."

"Thanks a lot, Jacob Two-Two."

S

skillick

In PEI, a "smidgeon." "Moira's new husband hasn't got a *skillick* of brains. He told her he forgot their anniversary because he thought it was on the 32nd of June."

skinner

In Newfoundland, someone whose job it is to remove the skin from seals or *fish*. "How many times am I *after* tellin' you, you don't need to *go down the road* lookin' for work as a *skinner*, because all the skinnin' jobs are right here."

skipper

In Newfoundland, 1) The master of a fishing boat. "*Skipper* says we need to move to new *grounds*." 2) The husband in a marriage. "Hey, *Skipper*, yer *missus* says yer grounded."

skookum

1) *Chinook jargon* for "strong," "big" or "powerful," from the Chehalis word "skukm" for power or bravery. "That's a *skookum* horse you've got there." 2) In more recent times, it is used in the West to mean "That's good" or "Cool."
"I got tickets to the 54-40 concert."
"*Skookum*."

skookum house

On the West Coast, slang for a jail or prison. "Did you see where Josh got drunk at the 54-40 concert and *beulahed* all over a cop and now he's in the *skookum house*."

S

skookum tum-tum

Intestinal fortitude, literally meaning "strong hearted," with "*tum-tum*" presumably referencing a heartbeat. "Now before you meet my brother-in-law, I'm bound to ask, have you got a *skookum tum-tum?*"

skookumchuck

Fast-moving water with a powerful current. "Don't fall in that *skookumchuck* or you'll get swept away."

slippy

In PEI, descriptive of a person thought to have criminal proclivities. "Don't trust Spud. He was born *slippy*."

slob ice

In the *Maritimes*, slushy, semi-solid ice.
"Well, Don, hockey season hasn't started yet, so let's comment on watching water freeze."
"It'll probably be more exciting than this year's *playoffs* were, Ron."
"Now it looks to me as if the water is starting to congeal over there. Would you call that *slob ice?*"
"Ron, at this point it's still just *frazil*. If it had already frozen and then it was thawing out, it would be *rotten ice*."
"You sure do know your *lolly*, Don."
"You know, Ron, I was right—watching water freeze **is** more exciting than the *playoffs*."

S

slocum

In PEI, a slow-moving or slow-thinking person. "Marge's nephew is a real *slocum*."
"What's he doin'?"
"I think he's chasin' his pet snail."

slumgullion

Suitable for use on the trail or at sea when referring to a thick, nearly solid stew made from whatever is available.
"Have you seen that bucket of *fish* heads I was saving for the cat? And where's my spare jar of molasses?"
"Here, try this pot of *slumgullion* I made."

slurry

In PEI, sludgy, mushy or watery ice. "Don't fall in the *slurry*."

Smarties

The brand name for candy available in Canada and other Commonwealth countries. Sold in boxes, *Smarties* consist of fat disks of chocolate about 1.5 centimetres in diameter and coated in a crisp (and usually colourful) candy coating. One of Canada's most memorable *Smarties* jingles began, "*When you eat your Smarties, do you eat the red ones last?*"

smoke up

To smoke marijuana. "Wanna go back in the *dooryard* and *smoke up?*"

snort

A slug or shot of hard liquor. "Will you have a *snort?*"

snotty

Descriptive of weather that is drizzly or wet. "It's a *snotty* day out there. Let's stay in."

snow broth

Very cold liquor. "We keep our *snow broth* cold in a bucket of *slurry*. Care for a *snort?*"

snow machine

Especially in rural areas, a snowmobile. "I'm takin' the *snow machine* into the *Co-op* for groceries. Need anything?" Americans living in Alaska and the northern states might also use this expression.

Snowbirds

1) Canada's famous military acrobatic flight demonstration team, whose official designation is "Canadian Forces 431 Demonstration Squadron." After accruing significant battle honours as a fighting squadron in World War II, the 431st was disbanded until 1954, when it was re-formed as both a working squadron and also an air-show squadron to showcase itself to the public. Since then, its duties have been limited to public displays and events. In their distinctive red and white CT-114 Tutor jets, the *Snowbirds* are famous for flying in tight formations and performing other difficult

S

manoeuvres. They received their name in the early 1970s when Gene McLellan's anthem of schmaltz, "Snowbird," sung by Anne Murray, was a popular radio staple. 2) Canadian senior citizens who winter in Florida.

snowmaggedon

A term coined late in 2008 for a series of harsh and voluminous snowstorms that partially buried parts of Ontario and Québec.

so thin they have to run around in the shower to get wet

In PEI, a colourful expression to describe someone who is extremely thin, the implication being that the subject is so slender that they could actually stand **between** the streams of water that issue from a shower head.

sonsy

In PEI, descriptive of a buxom or jolly woman, with "jolly" having its original meaning of "pleasingly rotund." "There's a *sonsy dilsey*."

(the) Soo

Short for Sault St. Marie, Ontario.

sooky baby

In the *Maritimes*, a person whose behaviour is childish or cowardly; a sissy or wimp. The double "o" in "sooky" rhymes with "book." When it is occasionally heard in other parts of Canada as well, "sucky" usually rhymes with "puppy." "Come on, it's just a bit of rain. No reason not to have a picnic. Don't be a *sooky baby*."

soother

A rubber nipple given to babies and infants to suck on. While the items themselves are common the world over, Canadians are more likely to call them *soothers* as opposed to "pacifiers," which is more common in the U.S. Both Canadians and Americans may use either term. "He's such a *sooky baby* sometimes I'm tempted to offer him a *soother*."

sorry

In Canada, the word *sorry* isn't so much an apology as an acknowledgement. For instance, you're walking along and a stranger accidentally treads on the back of your feet. In your moment of surprise, you're not really upset, just taken off-guard, and in Canada it is perfectly acceptable to blurt out *Sorry!* even though in these situations, technically, **you** are the one to whom *sorry* ought to be said. This and our shocking habit of actually thanking people for things give us our reputation for being polite.

south of 60

The areas of Canada below the 60th parallel. "Only people who live *south of 60* watch *North of 60*."

S

south of the border

An expression generally taken to mean "in the U.S." because the U.S. is south of Canada and the two countries share a border. "The plunging economy *south of the border* is dragging ours down with it."

spare

In Canadian high schools and universities, a block of time in which some students have no classes scheduled or are not required to be in class. *Spares* are when many Canadians sitting in the *caf* learn to play Euchre, drink pop and eat *ketchup-flavoured chips*.

Sparks Street, Ottawa

A former roadway in Ottawa, converted to a pedestrian footway in 1966, making it one of the first streets in North America to be so converted. However, it is included in this work because many Canadians will recognize the name from appeals to give charitably during commercial breaks on TV. For at least a decade in the 1970s (and sometimes still in 2008), *cheques* were to be sent to one of many different addresses on *Sparks Street*, all seemingly occupied by charities.

spinny

Crazy or foolish, often used to describe young women in their late teens or early twenties.

"When your sister was driving me to the store,

she told me that raccoons are really fairy bandits wearing masks."

"Yeah, she also calls them 'garbage imps.' She's definitely a bit *spinny*."

splice

In Newfoundland, to join others for drinking or to split the cost of a shared bottle of liquor. This term comes from the nautical term "splice," which means to weave the strands of two rope ends together, thus making one piece. "Let's *splice* up with our friends for a *snort* of *screech*."

spondulics

In western Canada of yore, "money." "This round's on me. I've got plenty of *spondulics*."

spread eagle/spread eagleism

In western Canada of yesteryear, prairie dwellers used this term to describe the tendency of our cousins *south of the border* to brag patriotically.

"Did Tex just call himself a God-Fearing, Gun-Toting 'Amurrkin'?"

"It did sound like he said, 'Amurrkin.'"

"Kind of a pungent whiff of *spread eagleism* wouldn't you say?"

spring break-up/spring thaw

A period during springtime when frozen bodies of water start to thaw, and the ice "breaks up." Canadians accustomed to long, hard winters often associate this time of year with a general

S

sense of relief after being cooped up indoors for months. Odd hijinks may occur during the *spring break-up*, as cabin-bound *Canucks* stretch their legs.

"Where was Jacques going with that jug of *caribou* and a *spudgel?*"

"Well, who knows? It's the *spring thaw* after all."

sprog

In PEI, a term for one's foot or shoe. Elsewhere in the world it may mean a small child (generally derogatory), a new military recruit or a small two-person dinghy-style sailboat. But in PEI, it means "feet" or "shoes." "Put up your *sprogs*," or "Kick off your *sprogs* and give your feet a rest."

Spud Island

In the rest of Canada, slang for "PEI" due to its famed potato crops.

"I'm going to visit my uncle on *Spud Island*."

"Make sure you take your *spurtle*."

spudgel

In Newfoundland, a bowl attached to a long handle used for single-handedly bailing out the bottom of one's boat.

"Water's comin' in somethin' fierce. Pass me the *spudgel*."

"I guess building my boat out of the bargain lumber wasn't such a great idea."

spurtle

In PEI, a wooden stick for stirring porridge.

"You put a bow on your *spurtle?*"
"Well, it's Christmas time—it's a festive *spurtle.*"

squid finger

In Newfoundland, swelling of the digits due to an allergic reaction to squid juice. "When I write my *Newfie* spy novel, I'm going to call the villain *Squid Finger*, and he's going to have a big swollen finger."
"What's his evil plot?"
"To increase of the value of his squid hoard by making the rest of the world's squid radioactive."

SRC

Societé Radio Canada. The French arm of the CBC.

St. John vs. St. John's

St. John is the largest city in New Brunswick and the oldest incorporated city in the North America. *St. John's* is the capital of Newfoundland. Many Canadians find it completely impossible to keep this straight, and many more are even unaware that there is a distinction. Be sure you enunciate clearly when booking plane tickets for either of these destinations, and better yet, always include the province after the city name.
"Hi, I'd like to get a ticket for *St. John's*, Newfoundland."
"Good thing you said 'Newfoundland,' because I can never keep the whole *St. John/St. John's* thing straight, and I might have booked you a ticket for New Brunswick instead."

"Considering you're a travel agent, isn't it important to keep that straight?"

"Well, a lot of people do get upset, but some of them can't tell the difference even when they get there."

St. Kitts
Short for the city of St. Catharines, Ontario.

stag and doe
A pre-wedding party that both men and women can attend as opposed to the more traditional "stag" party, which is for men only. Also called a "jack and jill" or even a "buck and doe."

Stanley Cup
1) The championship trophy of the NHL and the oldest professional sporting trophy in North America. Aside from the *Grey Cup*, it is the only pro-sports trophy whose possession is transferred from the last championship team to the next, instead of a new trophy being created every year for the winning team to keep. In 1888, Frederick Walter Stanley (a.k.a. Lord Stanley of Preston) was appointed Governor General of Canada. Over the next several years he and his 10(!) children became fervid hockey fans. At that time, although widely popular, hockey was only loosely organized, and Stanley wanted to encourage the creation of leagues. He decided to offer a trophy to be awarded each year to the top amateur team in Canada. Apparently, Lord Stanley felt that

nothing says "hockey league" like a silver... punchbowl. He duly ordered a nice one from a silversmith in England, and it was first awarded in 1894. Of course, over the intervening years, the Cup has come to be awarded for professional hockey. In order to accommodate the names of all the teams and players (from 1894 onward), it has sprouted a metre-tall base, allowing enough room for numerous engraved plates. This is the shape most familiar to hockey fans today. The Cup has also been the victim of several misadventures by victorious teams: in 1905, it was briefly lost after a member of the Ottawa Senators tried to drop kick it across the frozen Rideau Canal; in 1924, it was left by the side of the road after players on their way to a victory party had stopped to fix a flat tire; and in 1962, the *Maple Leafs* (after their last *Stanley Cup* victory, presumably 'til the end of time) managed to drop it into a bonfire where it was seriously damaged. 2) The series of playoff games to win the *Stanley Cup*. 3) The television broadcast of the various playoff games. "I'm watchin' the *Stanley Cup* tonight. Wanna come over?"

S

staving

In PEI, an intensifying adjective meaning "very." "*Lorsh*, but I'm drunk, *stavin'* drunk."

steamie

In Québec, a steamed *hot dog*. "Un *steamie* s'il vous plait." (A *steamie*, please.)

Steel City/Steeltown

Hamilton, Ontario, so-called for its predominant industry of steel production. *"I'm gonna go down the road to Steeltown."*

steppycock

In Newfoundland, a risky-sounding children's game of jumping from one *ice pan* to another in a "follow the leader" fashion. (See also *copy*.) *"Steppycock* is for neither the faint of heart nor the wobbly of ankle."

Stompin' Tom Connors

A Canadian songwriter, singer and guitar player whose peak of popularity was during the 1960s and 1970s, but who continues to record and perform at the time of this writing. Known for his playful and occasionally dreadful rhyming schemes, *Stompin' Tom* keeps time by stamping the heel of his boot on a piece of plywood (to protect the surface of the stage he's playing on). *Stompin' Tom's* subject matter is nothing less than the whole of Canada itself, and his repertoire includes such well-known songs as "Sudbury Saturday Night" (about the raucous carousing of the local inhabitants), "Bud the Spud" (about planting potatoes on PEI), "Big Joe Mufferaw" (about a giant, Paul Bunyan–like French Canadian *lumberjack*) and "The Hockey Song" (all about hockey). He is also notable for sending back his six Juno awards to protest the number of recipients who conduct most of their careers in the U.S., but who nonetheless received Canadian honours. His defining feature is genuine pride in Canada and Canadians.

(the) Strait
Short for "The Georgia Strait," a 240-kilometre-long channel of water between Vancouver Island (as well as the Gulf Islands) and mainland BC.

street hockey
(See *road hockey.*)

stubble jumper
In the Prairies, "a farmer," usually presumed to be from Saskatchewan. The term conjures to mind images of shorn grain fields and is gently derogatory, but nonetheless worn as a badge of pride by many Saskatchewanians.

stubbies/stubby (bottle)
From 1961 to 1986, Canadian beer came in short, fat bottles that were eventually phased out to make the sorting of returned empties easier. Many Canadians have a nostalgic fondness for *stubbies*, and some independent breweries are beginning to re-introduce them. "When we were younger, we used to go down to the park with a few *stubbies*, and once they were empty, we'd use them for target practice."

S

stuffed to the guppers

In PEI, to be full from eating. "*Lorsh*, after *Thanksgiving* dinner, I'm always *stuffed to the guppers*."

submarine races

When young couples drive off to a secluded spot overlooking a body of water (a promising location for osculation), they are said to be watching the *submarine races*. The absence of any nearby bodies of water is usually not a deterrent to the enjoyment of this very participatory spectator sport.

"Where's your big brother?"

"He said he was going to watch the *submarine races*."

"That's how I met your father."

"But we live in Saskatchewan. Where do the submarines go to race?"

sudden death

In hockey, an extra period (*OT*) called when two teams are tied and in which the first team to score wins the game.

sugar bush

A grove of *maple* trees from which *maple syrup* can be produced. "I'm off to tap some trees in the *sugar bush*."

sugar shack

A small hut or stand in a *sugar bush*, where traditional dishes flavoured or garnished with *maple syrup* are served. "If you're good, we can go to the *sugar shack* this afternoon."

sugar tea
In Newfoundland, tea sweetened with sugar as opposed to molasses, and served on special occasions. "It's your birthday, so no *bare-legged* or *switchel* for you. It's *sugar tea* 'til day's end."

sunburn
In hockey, a condition said to affect goalies who are frequently scored upon. When a goal is scored, a red light mounted at the end of rink, behind the goal, comes on and "burns" the back of the goalie's neck. "Well, I'm sad to say it, but the home team's goalie is getting a bad case of *sunburn* today."

sunburst
A halo-like trimming of fur around the hood of a parka.

Sunshine Coast
The southwestern coast of BC, especially north of Howe Sound on the Strait of Georgia, in reference to the relative absence of permanent cloud cover in this area.

Super, Natural BC
An irritating, but well-remembered advertising slogan encouraging tourists to visit BC's many attractions.

S

sweat lodge

Tents or huts used by some Aboriginal groups to induce sweating for medicinal or religious purposes. Traditionally, stones were heated in a fire and then moved into the *sweat lodge*, where water was poured over them to create steam (in much the same way as a sauna). As well as sweating out toxins and sickness, *sweat lodges* are also used to assist with meditation.

swish

In the *Maritimes*, liquor made by filling a newly empty rum barrel with boiling water and then literally rotating the barrel every few days for a number of weeks until the barrel staves have yielded their alcoholic goodness. "It's been a pretty lean couple of months, but I can offer you a glass of *swish*."

switchel

In Newfoundland, weak tea sweetened with molasses, and without milk, usually drunk by fishermen and sealers. "It's a cold one today. Here, have a cup of *switchel* to thaw you out a bit."

T. Dot/T.O.

Both slang terms for "Toronto."

Tabernac! (pron: tab-arr-NAK)

A *sacré* referencing the tabernacle of a church and never far from the lips of stereotypical *voyageurs*, fur trappers and French Canadians, especially in cartoons. "Le *dépanneur* est fermé. *Tabernac!*" (The convenience store is closed. *Tabernacle!*)

tailor-made

Used to describe commercially-made cigarettes as opposed to those rolled by hand (rollies). "Might I prevail upon you for one of your fine *tailor-mades?* I've run out of tobacco."

Take off

1) A euphemism immortalized by the *McKenzie Brothers*, both in their *Great White North* segments on *SCTV* and on their hit album, also called *Great White North*. It is properly followed by *eh*, all spoken in the tone of an annoyed command rather than an actual question: "*Take off, eh?*" While it is no secret that *Take off* is a watered-down form of

"f**k off," its intensity is also watered down and, in some situations, may simply mean "stop bugging me."

"Hey, I checked, and a pound of *back bacon* does **not** equal 32 kilos."

"*Take off, eh?*"

2) A hit novelty song from the *Great White North* album, sung by Geddy Lee of the band Rush, and whose main lyric was "*Take off! Take off* to the *Great White North/* It's a *beauty* way to go."

talk the nuts off a steel bridge

A backroads "bon mot" to describe someone whose mouth runneth over.

"Your brother-in-law cornered me at the bar last night and started tellin' me all about his new *snow machine*."

"He could *talk the nuts off a steel bridge*."

tap

What Americans are more apt to call a "faucet," Canadians call a *tap*; that is, a pressurized spigot that water comes out of, usually found in kitchens and bathrooms.

"You left the *tap* running and now the *Arborite*'s ruined."

"You mean I left the faucet running and ruined the melamine counter?"

"Pick one, *Yankee*."

tea

In Newfoundland, the evening meal, especially

when eaten on a fishing boat or whaler, but certainly in the home as well. In other parts of Canada, it is "supper" or "dinner."

"Time for *tea*."

"*Tea?* I'm starving—shouldn't we have supper?"

"That's what I said—time for *tea*."

tea towel

A thin cotton or linen towel for drying dishes, more likely to be called a "dish towel" in the U.S.

"Grab a *tea towel*, and dry the dishes."

Tensor bandage

A brand name of wide, usually brown, *elastic* bandages that are wrapped tightly around joints to provide support.

"This first aid teacher really talks a lot, *eh?*"

"Yup. Too bad we don't have some kind of *elastic* binding to wrap tightly around his head and shut him up."

"Well, pass me that *Tensor bandage*."

Terry Fox Run

An annual, one-day running event to raise money for cancer research, usually held on the second Sunday after Labour Day. It is named for Terry Fox, who ran more than 5000 kilometres across Canada during his "Marathon of Hope" in 1980. After losing his right leg to cancer, Terry was fitted with a prosthetic limb and crossed nearly half of Canada with his determined hopping gait. He succumbed to the cancer before he could finish

315

the journey and died one month short of his 22nd birthday. Today he is remembered as a Canadian hero and a figure of inspiration to people around the world.

thank you

Like *please*, the unthinking use of this phrase frequently distinguishes Canadian travellers from American tourists, especially in U.S. itself and other English-speaking countries.

Thanksgiving

1) A statutory holiday (except in New Brunswick, Nova Scotia and PEI, where it may be a holiday but is not statutory) celebrated in Canada on the second Monday in October. In Canada, *Thanksgiving* has much the same cultural significance as it does *south of the border*: a long weekend, football on TV and time with family and friends. 2) A *blanket* term for the entire long weekend as opposed to the day itself. "Are you going home for *Thanksgiving?*" Because it is celebrated later in the U.S. (the fourth Thursday in November), the term *Thanksgiving* can often cause confusion when Canadians and Americans have business dealings together. In these cases, it is appropriate to insert "Canadian" or "American" before *Thanksgiving*. "It's American *Thanksgiving* this weekend. We won't hear from them for the rest of the week."

the hurrier I go, the behinder I get

A folksy colloquialism meaning: "The more

I hurry, the more I fall behind."

"You seem to have put your socks on **over** your shoes."

"Darn! I was rushing so I won't be late for the *logging bee*, but I guess *the hurrier I go, the behinder I get.*"

them (days, times)

In Newfoundland, *them* can specify a time relatively long ago, perhaps during the speaker's lifetime, perhaps before.

"Things were different when we were growing up."

"*Them* days you could go to a movie for a nickel and still have change for popcorn."

there's no grain in that silo

An agricultural metaphor to describe someone seen to be lacking in intelligence.

"Did you see where Marge's husband poured bacon fat down the drain and then when it got clogged, he decided to try to clear it out with hot wax?"

"*There's no grain in that silo.*"

there's nowhere that'll go in a day

In PEI, an expression sometimes heard in acknowledgement that a vehicle is really and truly out of commission for the foreseeable future.

"Well, the transmission's fallen out, the carburetor's on the fritz, and the whole car is up on blocks. What do you think?"

"*There's nowhere that'll go in a day.*"

T

317

This Hour Has Seven Days

A groundbreaking weekly news magazine program that ran on *CBC* TV from 1964 to 1966. A panel of reporters tackled issues of the day (ranging from capital punishment to sex scandals) through hard-hitting interviews, sketches and satirical songs. The hosts often also surprised interview subjects outside their homes and conducted brief interviews, for which the subjects were woefully unprepared. The mixture of hard news reporting with satirical "entertainment" elements was controversial as was the program's tendency to report on social issues that were not considered appropriate topics for discussion in polite company.

This Hour Has 22 Minutes

A satirical mock-news comedy show running from 1993 to the time of this writing. Its title is partly a nod to *This Hour Has Seven Days* and also the fact that half-hour TV shows only have 22 minutes of actual content because of advertising breaks. Among other things, *This Hour Has 22 Minutes* also borrows the tradition of surprising public figures and getting them to do or say ridiculous things (such as getting Reform Party Leader Preston Manning to helplessly attempt the ignition of a child-proof lighter, which he couldn't, even after presenter Rick Mercer repeatedly showed him where the safety button was). Another famous segment involved Mercer

T

conducting "streeter" interviews with Americans, leading them to say ridiculous things about Canada, in a segment called "Talking to Americans." (See *igloo.*)

This tastes like more
A homey way of saying, "This food is good."
"How do you like my *Nanaimo bars?*"
"*These taste like more.*"

those (days)
In Newfoundland, a term denoting "today" or the "present" (in most other places in Canada it is "these" days). "*Those* days everything's so much more expensive than *them* days."

throat singing
An *Inuit* custom that is practiced more as a game than a musical performance. The singers stand opposite each other, and one begins vocalizing a rhythmic sound with spaces between the "beats" that the other participant fills in. Typically these sessions might last for two or three minutes until one of the participants laughs, runs out of breath or simply can't make the sound anymore. Traditionally, it was practiced by women to pass the time while their men were away on fishing trips. Sometimes one singer moves very close in order to use the other's open mouth as a resonating chamber, making for even more unusual sounds.

T

319

throater

In the Newfoundland fishing industry, a member of the shore crew who cuts the throats of *fish* and slits their bellies open.

"My work experience? Well, *them* days I was a *shaker*, then I was an *elbow picker*, then I was *after goin' down the road* and worked *hangin' kill* and *shakin' stick* and then I came back to *The Rock*, but I got *squid finger* at my last job and so *those* days I'm a *throater*."

throughother

In PEI, descriptive of a house or room in disorder. "Oh, this is my son's room—don't look in there—it's all *throughother*."

thunder jug/thunder mug

In PEI, 1) A jug for alcohol, usually spirits. "I'm thirsty and it's New Year's Eve; pass me the *thunder jug*." 2) In days of yore, a chamber pot. "It's New Year's Day and I need to *beulah*; pass the *thunder jug*."

tight as two coats of paint

In PEI, a colourful but rarely heard phrase describing two objects with little room between them. "Oh, *Lorsh*, look at my brother and his girlfriend canoodling in the corner; *tight as two coats of paint*."

tikinagan

An Inuktitut word for the thin plank of wood

traditionally used by mothers to carry their babies on their backs.

Tim Hortons (a.k.a. Tim's/Timmy Ho's)

A chain of restaurants specializing in coffee, donuts, soups and sandwiches, considered by many Canadians to be emblematic of Canada. Tim Horton was an NHL hockey player who opened a small shop selling *doughnuts* and coffee in Hamilton, Ontario, in 1964. He soon acquired a business partner, Ron Joyce who, upon Horton's death in 1974, took over the chain and aggressively expanded it. Today, *Tim Hortons* franchises are all across Canada, although there are fewer in Manitoba and Saskatchewan than elsewhere. The brand is also very popular with Canadian Armed Forces personnel and most bases have a *Tim's* nearby. At the time of this writing, there is even a *Tim's* in a 40-foot trailer at the Canadian Forces base in Kandahar, Afghanistan. A popular TV advertising campaign showed vignettes of Canadians travelling abroad who missed *Tim Hortons*. The chain's annual *Roll Up the Rim to Win* promotion is notorious. It is also likely (but cannot be proven) that the noted Canadianism, *double-double*, originated at a *Tim Hortons*.

"I'm goin' to *Tim's*. Want anything?"

"Can you get me a medium *double-double* and a *raised chocolate?*"

TimBits

The brand name of small spherical *doughnuts* sold by *Tim Hortons* and known outside of the *Tim's* universe as "*doughnut* holes" since they are about the size of the hole in a *doughnut*, or, for those not up on their *doughnut* lore, the size of a golf ball. *TimBits* come in a variety of flavours and, while they can be bought singly, are usually ordered by the dozen. They are also a popular treat for office workers to bring for one another, especially on Fridays or when someone arrives late at a meeting.

"You're late."

"I brought *TimBits*…"

tin

While Canadians will say either *tin* or "can" when referring to a cylindrical metal container, Americans are more likely to use only "can." Canadians most often use *tin* when referring to the puck-shaped containers that flaked tuna or salmon come in.

"I need a can of beans and a *tin* of tuna."

"Whatever you're making, I don't want any."

tintamarre

A noisy parade, especially on National Acadian Day, August 15.

toboggan

A small sleigh with an upward, rear-curling front, used for sliding down snow-covered hills at enjoyably high speeds. *Toboggans* can generally hold one or two adults or up to three children. Variants of the word pop up in both the Algonquian and Micmac dialects.

tobogganing

The act of riding on a *toboggan*. "Let's go *tobogganing*."

toonie (twonie)

Canada's two-dollar coin, called a *toonie* (or twonie) to rhyme with *loonie*. When the coins were introduced, a variety of other nicknames were floated, including the piratical sounding "doubloon," being a combination of "double" and "loon." Since the coin features the Queen on one side and a polar bear on the obverse, one punster dubbed it "The Queen with a bear (bare) behind."

toonik

1) An Inuktitut term usually rendered as "tuniq" or "tunit." The *tooniks* were a primitive culture who lived in Canada's arctic before the *Inuit*. The *Inuit* regarded the *tooniks* as a mysterious race of shy giants who were easily frightened off. Archeologists classify them as a "Paleo-Eskimo" group, also called the "Dorset Culture." 2) A non-human creature in *Inuit* mythology, probably derived from legends about the "tunits." 3) A sealskin doll made by *Inuit* artisans as a souvenir. These keepsake *tooniks* have red eyes, pot bellies and long

T

fangs. They are different in form, but comparable in purpose to an *ookpik*.

Toonik Tyme

A springtime festival established in 1965 by community leaders in Iqaluit (then Frobisher Bay). *Toonik Tyme*'s purpose was twofold: first, to celebrate the return of the sun after the long, dark months of winter; and, second, to encourage tourism in the North. Nowadays, *Toonik Tyme* is generally celebrated in April and features entertainers, artisans and competitions. With a mixture of traditional and modern attractions, it is a favourite and much anticipated time of year in the North.

"What are you sharpening your *ooloo* for?"

"I'm getting ready for the seal-skinning contest at *Toonik Tyme*."

toupie (pron: TOO-pee)

A round, boneless smoked ham, possibly from "toupie," French for "spinning top," because of the ham's shape.

"Pass the *toupie*, please."

"We call them toupées here, buddy, and we don't share them, especially at the dinner table."

toutin/touton (pron: TOO-tin)

In Newfoundland, 1) A deep-fried round bread (similar in size and shape to a pancake) often eaten for breakfast. "Pull up a chair and put a couple of *toutons* on your plate." 2) A bun made with flour, molasses and bits of pork. In the olden days, *toutons* were a popular food for woodsmen because, if they had enough pork in them, they would not freeze as often as other foods. "I'm going to get a fire going and heat up my *touton*."

TransCanada Highway

A highway connecting all 10 of Canada's provinces, begun in 1950 and completed in 1971. At 7821 kilometres, it is the third longest highway in the world after the Trans Siberian Highway and Australia's Highway 1. Distinctive signs showing a white *maple leaf* on a green background mark the way. For many Canadians, driving from one side of the country to the other on the *TransCanada Highway* is an incidental rite of passage— incidental because usually the trip is for a reason (wedding, holidays, vacation, and so on).

tree planting

A process in which private forestry firms hire workers to plant seedlings in areas that have been cleared by logging. For many Canadians of university age, *tree planting* is a strenuous but lucrative way to earn money over the summer for university tuition and living expenses. In some ways it can be thought of as an "extreme summer job," with tree planters living in small groups in remote areas, often clear-cut mountainsides. Workdays are 8–10 hours long, and planters bend over more than 200 times per hour.

325

Living facilities are spartan, usually tents or other portable structures, and daily amenities like running water are usually in short supply. "I was thinking of either joining the military or going *tree planting*. I'm still not sure which one will be more difficult."

triple-triple
When ordering coffee, to ask for three creams and three sugars. Undoubtedly, this phrase is an extension of *double-double*. "Can I get one medium *triple-triple*, please?" (see also *four by four*)

Trudeau salute
A raised middle finger, also known as "flipping the bird." This offensive gesture was so-called in Canada, because Prime Minister Pierre Trudeau once flashed it through the window of a train to an on-looking group of reporters, photographers and television journalists.

Trudeaumania
Widespread personal fascination and support for Pierre Trudeau during the 1968 federal election that made him prime minister for the first time.

true north strong and free
A line from "*O Canada*," referencing Canada itself and sometimes used on its own as patriotic slang. "I can't wait to get back to the *true north strong and free* once my tour of duty's over."

tum-tum
Chinook jargon for one's heart, both literally and

figuratively. Although it sounds like it should stand for "tummy," *tum-tum* is probably an onomatopoeic reference to the sound of a heart beating. "You are brave; you have a *skookum tum-tum*."

tundra

An area with a substrate of permafrost and limited tree growth due to chilly temperatures and a short growing season. It occurs in sub-polar regions of Canada, Russia and parts of Alaska. Its vast, treeless expanses are generally flat plains, and so *tundra* is seen as characterizing Canada's sprawling, wild and sometimes bleak nature.
"On Canadian reality shows, they should send the losers to the *tundra*."
"*Lorsh*, most times I wish they'd banish the winners."

Tundra Buggy

The commercial name of a large vehicle used to transport tourists across stretches of snowy *tundra*, often in the hope of spying polar bears or other wildlife. They have huge wheels and fairly large cabins. Were it not so military-sounding, "tundra tank" might be a more accurate name.

tuque

A dome- or cone-shaped, knitted woollen cap (with or without a small pom-pom on top) seen by some Canadians as being emblematic of their home and native land. The origins of the word are contentious. It may come from the French name for the hat—"toque"—itself derived from "toquer," meaning "to knock," since prototype "toques" were long and droopy with ends that knocked their wearer's backs. Or, it may come from the pre-Latin word "tukka" for "hill" or "mound," presumably referencing the hat's shape. Finally, *tuque* may originate in the *Chinook jargon* word "latuk," meaning "woollen cap."

"The other *CBC* executives and I would like you to come up with two extra minutes of distinctly Canadian content for the show's Canadian broadcast."

"But for the last two years the show's been written and produced in Canada with a cast and crew of Canadians."

"Nonetheless— "

"Okay, fine—bring me a couple of parkas, some boxes of beer, a few pounds of back bacon and a sign that says *Great White North*, and we'll give you your *CanCon*. Oh, and send Wardrobe over with a couple of *tuques* too."

Tweed Curtain

In BC, especially on Vancouver Island, the cultural divide seen as separating the district of Oak Bay (full of Edwardian buildings and so perceived as being very British or "tweedy") from the rest of Victoria. It is an obvious play on the metaphorical "Iron Curtain," said to separate Soviet Russia from the rest of the world during the Cold War.

"Who knows what goes on behind the *Tweed Curtain?*"

twenty-sixer

A 26-ounce bottle of liquor.

"I'm goin' to the liquor store. Do you want me to pick you up a *twenty-sixer* or a *forty-pounder* for the *May two-four weekend?*"

"Just a *twenty-sixer*. I'm trynna take it easy."

twist/twister

In Newfoundland, a hand-rolled cigarette, as opposed to a commercially made cigarette.

"I scoff at your *tailor-mades* and opt instead for a *twist*."

"You weren't scoffing when you ran out of rolling papers."

"No, that's true, I wasn't."

two-four

A case of beer containing 24 bottles or cans. In Canada, one or more *two-fours* are must-have purchases for long weekends, camping trips and parties. For non-beer drinkers seeking to avoid social embarrassment, if you are standing in line at the beer store and notice that everyone in front of you is ordering *two-fours*, you may want to reconsider ordering that six-pack of wine coolers.

Two Solitudes

1) The title of a 1945 novel by Hugh MacLennan, which focused on the lack of communication and

interaction between Canada's French and English cultures. 2) A phrase used in subsequent years to describe the cultural distance between English and French Canada.

tyee
Chinook jargon for 1) "chief" as in "tribal chief": "She is the *hyas tyee*." 2) "superior" as in "better than": "That's a *tyee chic chic* you've got there." As such, in BC it is a popular name for business, being more or less the Chinook equivalent of "A-1"; for instance, *Tyee* Building Supplies, *Tyee* Montessori School, *Tyee* Storm & Drain, and so on. 3) A spring salmon weighing more than 13.5 kilograms.

T

UIC

Short for Unemployment Insurance Commission and usually further shortened to just "UI." Although it has since been supplanted by the more politically correct *Employment Insurance Commission* (maybe if we don't call it unemployment it will go away), or *EI* for short, the organization's function remains the same, and many people still call it *UI* instead of *EI* anyway.

UIC ski team

In BC, especially during the 1980s, people who were adept at both collecting their *UI* benefits and staying loose on the slopes.

"How is it you can always be out here skiing? Don't any of you have jobs?"

"We used to have jobs, but now we're on the *UIC ski team*."

umiak

The Inuktitut name for an open, flat-bottomed boat traditionally used by *Inuit* women. The word means literally "woman's boat," while the more familiar "kayak" means "man's boat." A large *umiak* may be as long as 10 metres and can hold up to 20 people. It is made by stretching animal hide (usually seal or walrus) over a wooden frame, though metal frames are often used today. "I'm thinking of introducing *umiak* races at *Toonik Tyme*. Will you be on my team?"

up at crow piss

In PEI, a euphemism for getting up early.

"What're you yawning for? It's only lunch time."

"I was *up at crow piss* this morning."

up the stump

A rather unpleasant-sounding BC expression meaning "pregnant."

"I haven't seen your sister at one of these logging dances for a long time."

"She danced with one logger too many; she's *up the stump*."

upalong

In Newfoundland, an oft-heard phrase meaning "far away," especially of Newfoundlanders who have gone to other parts of Canada or abroad.

"All my friends are *upalong*. I miss them."

Upper Canada

A British colony that existed in present-day southern Ontario from 1791 to 1841. It has many namesakes and cultural references, including but not limited to *Upper Canada* College (founded in

1829), *Upper Canada* Mall (opened in 1974) and the *Upper Canada* Brewing Company (brewing since 1984).

Upper Canada Rebellion

An 1837 rebellion that took place in Toronto with disgruntled farmers marching against unfair land allocation and citing a number of other grievances. Led by William Lyon Mackenzie, the rebellion itself was a complete flop; a number of the instigators were arrested, hanged or, in Mackenzie's case, went into exile in the U.S. The armed conflict, however brief and ineffectual, did get the attention of the British government, who assigned Lord Durham to investigate. His report and recommendations helped pave the way for the union of Upper and *Lower Canada* (heretofore mere colonies) into the Province of Canada in 1840.

Va pèter dans le trèfle

In Québec, a cryptic but effective insult that translates literally as "Go fart in the clover."

"That's your mother-in-law? I thought it was the *loup-garou!*"

"*Va pèter dans le trèfle!*"

Van Groovy

A jocular name for Vancouver due to the city's perceived mellow pace of life; also, no doubt, in reference to the easy availability of *BC Bud*. It joins a long list of silly place names for Canadian cities.

"This Christmas I'm flying from *Van Groovy* to *Hogtown* and then on to *The Rock.*"

"You'll fly over *Edmonchuk, the Jaw* and *Winterpeg.*"

"That's some seriously unnecessary but nonetheless amusing exposition."

"I try."

Varsol

A brand name of paint thinner sold in Canada. Its name is a contraction of "varnish makers' solvent." It can also be used as a derogatory simile when talking about an alcoholic beverage having a bad flavour.

"What kind of wine is this? It tastes like *Varsol!*"

"It's homemade; I call it Château *AlCan.*"

vendu

A *Québecois* who has assimilated into *anglo* culture or "sold out." The word means "sold" in French.

Vi-Co

In Saskatchewan, a brand name of chocolate milk.

Victoria Day

A holiday in honour of Queen Victoria's birthday (May 24), which is observed on the Monday immediately preceding May 25. (See also *May two-four weekend.*)

(The) Voice of Doom

Many Canadians remember actor Lorne Greene as either Ben "Pa" Cartwright on the U.S. TV western *Bonanza* (1959–73) or as Adama from the first incarnation of the U.S. sci-fi series *Battlestar Galactica* (1978–79). However, from 1939 to 1942, the Ottawa-born Greene was also the principal newsreader for *CBC* radio. The network billed him as the "Voice of Canada," but after Canada entered World War II and news stories were dominated by death and destruction, many listeners dubbed him *The Voice of Doom.*

voyageur

1) French for "traveller," this term refers to one of the legendary *coureurs de bois* whose specialty was expertly paddling large canoes laden with fur pelts along rivers and across lakes to the storehouses of Montréal merchants. Most *voyageurs* held permits from Montréal fur traders to distinguish themselves from unlicensed and less reliable employees. Mainly French Canadian, *Métis* or members of the *First Nations*, *voyageurs* were renowned for their nearly superhuman strength and endurance; they could paddle at 55 strokes per minute (if not more), were capable of carrying two 40-kilogram (90-pound) bundles of fur over lengthy *portages* and generally undertook these strenuous activities for 14 hours per day. With their heyday between 1680 and 1800, the *voyageurs* are today celebrated as folk heroes (see *Chasse-galerie* and *Maudit!)* and symbolize the supposedly tough, jolly and hardworking temperament that our environment has foisted upon us. For non-Canadians, especially Europeans, *voyageur* and *lumberjacks* may be the first two stereotypes that leap to mind when Canada is mentioned. 2) A popular name for businesses in Canada, especially those to do with travel or leisure; for example, *Voyageur* White Water Rafting, *Voyageur* Bait and Tackle, *Voyageur* Family Restaurant, *Voyageur* Colonial Bus Lines.

waffle stompers

In BC, hiking boots with coarse, cleated treads that leave a distinctive waffle-textured footprint.

"Is this a *Sasquatch* footprint?"

"No, brainiac, it's a hiker-wearing-*waffle-stompers* footprint."

walk a cat

In BC and elsewhere, to drive a bulldozer from one site to another under its own power (as opposed to towing it on a trailer). Industry slang for bulldozer is "cat" because of their metal-linked treads called "**cat**erpillar" treads. This is another expression sure to cause confusion not just for non-Canadians, but also for those unfamiliar with "heavy duty" slang.

"I gotta go *walk a cat*."

"You're leaving the construction site to take your pet for a constitutional? Wow, you folks sure do things differently up here in Canada."

wampum

1) Among *First Nations* peoples, *wampum* was both the singular and plural form for beads made from

the polished inner surfaces of various shells, usually having an attractive pearl-like lustre. *Wampum* beads and belts were used for currency and trade between *First Nations* individuals and tribes as well as between the *First Nations* and Europeans. "I'll trade you this *wampum* belt for this gun." *Wampum* of differing colour was also used as a pledge of friendship and as an offering to mark solemn occasions: white *wampum* stood for health, friendship and peace, while black or purple *wampum* might be given on a sad occasion calling for sympathy and sorrow. 2) Porcelain beads introduced by Europeans for trading purposes and called *wampum* by both Aboriginal and European traders. 3) Modern-day slang for "money," usually used in a joking manner. "The people up in payroll must have stayed up late; they actually managed to have your *wampum* ready on time for a change."

washboard

Descriptive of the ungraded dirt roads found in so many rural areas across North America and so-called for the regular, undulating ridges (similar to the ridges on a washboard) that form from being driven over by many vehicles.
"What is that sound?"
"It's my teeth knocking together from driving on this *washboard* road!"

Wayne & Shuster

A comedy duo (Johnny Wayne, 1918–90, and Frank Shuster, 1916–2002) active from the late

1940s to the late 1980s. While their approach was far more conceptual than vaudevillian, in some ways they can be thought of as Canada's Abbot & Costello. They appeared on *The Ed Sullivan Show* a record 67 times in 11 years, and despite many offers to base themselves *south of the border*, opted to remain a strictly Canadian act. *Wayne & Shuster* worked in radio, TV and performed live extensively, both overseas (for Allied troops during World War II) and here at home. Some of their most famous routines included re-imagining Shakespeare's "Julius Caesar" as a modern-day murder investigation; a baseball routine involving characters from Hamlet and Macbeth; as well as the ever-popular "Frontier Psychiatrist," in which a Viennese psychiatrist tries to bring mental health to the Wild West ("There's no such things as villains; just problem cowboys.") They were an influence on most Canadian comedy acts that followed and are fondly remembered.

Were you born in a sawmill?

In PEI, a woodsy way of asking, "Have you no manners?"

"I stir my tea with my thumb."

"Were you born in a sawmill?!"

"Yes, I was, actually. Why do you think they call me 'Born-in-a-sawmill-Bjorn'?!"

Wetcoast

Slang for Canada's west coast, because of the

frequent rain and cloudy weather. (See also *Don't like the weather? Just wait five minutes*.) "I'm goin' to the *Wetcoast* to visit my sister."

Wetcoast Samsonite

In BC's coastal region, green plastic garbage bags filled with clothes used by frequent passengers on float planes and favoured because they are not only waterproof but can be squashed into small spaces with relative ease. "That suitcase'll never fit on the plane; you're better off using *Wetcoast Samsonite*."

When you eat your Smarties, do you eat the red ones last?

The first line of a *Smarties* jingle seared into the minds of two generations of *Smarties* lovers from the mid-1970s to the mid-1990s. The jingle, in its entirety goes:

When you eat your Smarties, do you eat the red ones last?

Do you suck them very slowly or crunch them very fast?

Eat those candy-coated chocolates, but tell me when I ask,

When you eat your Smarties, do you eat the red ones last?

While most people cannot remember the third line, many Canadians upon seeing a friend eating *Smarties* will still blurt out, *"When you eat your Smarties, do you eat the red ones last?* Do you suck them very slowly or crunch them very fast?"

where God buried his socks

A remote location, probably not very developed. "Where's this wedding rehearsal we have to go to on the weekend?"

"It's *where God buried his socks* is where it is."

whistle punk

In logging lingo of yore, a *whistle punk* was a boy who blew a whistle to alert the *donkeyman* that a distant load of logs had been secured together by the *hooktender,* and the *donkeyman* could now start the engine to haul the logs.

whitewashed American

In PEI, an expression to describe a Canadian who has gone to live in the U.S. and puts on American airs.

"Lord Black may have once been Canadian, but now he's a *whitewashed American.*"

"If Lord Black heard you say that, he'd call you a mendacious popinjay."

"While he himself is a sententious bloviant."

Who peed in your cornflakes this morning?

A colloquialism meaning "Why are you in such a bad mood?" more or less equivalent to "Who ran over your puppy this morning?"

wild-and-woolly

In its strictest sense, this friendly sounding phrase is descriptive of uncouth or untamed behaviour, possibly because early pioneers wore their wool-lined coats with the wool turned outwards (why they would do this remains unclear since leaving it turned inwards would certainly be warmer). But when used today, it is generally used to describe rambunctious goings-on ("My two adolescent sons have set a new standard for *wild-and-woolly* behaviour.") or to suggest something that might generally be seen as improper or at least disapproved of by parents. "There were some *wild-and-woolly* doings after prom night this year."

windrow

A row of snow that has been left along the side of the road by a *plough* or grader. *Windrows* are the bane of many a Canadian's winter, because, after heavy snowfalls, they can be a metre or more tall and create a mountainous obstruction at the end of recently shovelled driveways in both rural and urban communities.

Winnipeg General Strike of 1919

An infamous strike in which more than 30,000 workers walked off the job to protest their poor wages and lack of collective bargaining rights. Winnipeg was then a city of just 175,000 and so the strike had a considerable impact. The Conservative government of Robert Borden cravenly attempted to paint the strike as the result of an international Bolshevik conspiracy and also sent the *North West Mounted Police* to break up a gathering on June 17, later known as "Bloody Saturday"

because it resulted in one death and 30 injuries. Several of the instigators were sentenced to jail terms, some were deported and one voluntarily left for exile in the U.S. The forces of organized labour in Canada turned against the Conservatives, and they were trounced in the following election. The incoming Liberal government under William Lyon Mackenzie King opted to enact the reforms recommended by the Royal Commission looking into the strike, but it would be another 30 years before unionization and collective bargaining would become the right of all workers.

Winterlude
A winter carnival usually held during the first three weeks of February in Ottawa, Ontario, and Gatineau, Québec. There are the expected ice sculptures and skating as well as numerous other entertainments and attractions.

Winterpeg
Slang for Winnipeg, due to its infamously cold and snowy weather. "If you go to *Winterpeg*, be sure to have your picture taken at *Portage and Main*, but try not to get blown over."

Wobbly
A nickname for any member of the International Workers of the World (IWW), possibly originating, and most often used, in Canada. One theory among several about the origins of this term is that, in 1911, the proprietor of a Chinese restaurant in

Vancouver, unable to pronounce the "l" sound in the "double-u" of "IWW," instead produced the sounds "Eye Wobbly Wobbly." Customers who showed him their red membership card were given free credit. The IWW website proudly proclaims that this version could be true since the IWW was the first such organization not to discriminate against Asian immigrant workers. The nickname seems to have been used both as a noun—"Are you a *wobbly?*"—and an adjective—"Are you *wobbly?*"

Wouldn't that frost your preserves!/fluff your feathers!

In PEI, an exclamation of amazement, roughly equivalent to "Well, if that doesn't take the cake!" or "Well, I'll be darned!" "Look at this headline: 'Local Potato Tycoon Goes *Wobbly*'! *Wouldn't that frost your preserves!*"

Wrestling Day

In Williams Lake, BC, a holiday observed on January 2 of each year in a flippant echo of "Boxing Day." In the 1930s, local merchants Syd Western and Alistair McKenzie noticed that business on January 2 was next to non-existent and so decided to close their stores for an extra holiday that they dubbed *Wrestling Day*. Declared an official civic holiday in 1978, it has been celebrated ever since.

Yankees/Yanks

A contemptuous term for Americans, the intensity of which ranges from non-existent to rabid. It can be heard in most English-speaking Commonwealth countries.

Yoho blow

In BC, a strong wind that travels down the Kicking Horse Valley in Yoho National Park. "Yoho" is a Cree word to express amazement.

york

To throw up. "Look, I'll give you a ride home, but just don't *york* in my car."

you can't keep a good dog off your leg

In PEI, an expression to indicate obstinacy.
"Even though I always say no, he still calls me every week to see if I'll go out on a date with him."
"Well, *you can't keep a good dog off your leg.*"

Z

Zamboni

The brand name of a machine that smoothes rough ice between the periods of hockey games. A *Zamboni* looks like a giant riding lawn mower, and even though other companies make similar ice resurfacing machines, the *Zamboni* has become the Kleenex of the ice resurfacing world, with its proper brand name often used in reference to generic products of similar ilk. Invented by—who else—Frank Zamboni, the first model appeared in 1949.

"Why is there a futuristic looking tractor on the ice?"

"That's the *Zamboni*."

zed

The last letter of the alphabet, as opposed to the American pronunciation "zee." Despite this, many Canadian business and products still follow the U.S. example of calling themselves "E-Z" for "easy," much to the frustration of right-thinking Canadians.

"Hello, this is E-Zee Carpet and Flooring. How may I help you?"

"It's E-*Zed* actually."

"Sorry?"

"The name of your company is E-*Zed*."

"I can assure you that our company's name is E-Zee."

"It's the letter 'E' followed by the letter 'Z,' which is pronounced *zed* in Canada, thank you very much."

zut alors

A mild French curse, roughly equivalent to "Damn it!" Although it is not a specifically French Canadian curse, it is often found in Canadian school primers as a mild curse, and die-hard *anglos* often use it is a joking swear. "My tea has gone cold and my crumpets have burnt—*zut alors!*"

Notes on Sources

Print

Avis, Walter S., ed. in chief. *A Dictionary of Canadianisms on Historical Principles*. Toronto: W.J. Gage Limited, 1967.

—"So *eh?* Is Canadian, eh?" *The Canadian Journal of Linguistics*, 17 (1972): 89–104.

Barber, Katherine, ed. in chief. *The Canadian Oxford Dictionary, 2nd Ed*. Don Mills: Oxford University Press, 2004.

Barber, Katherine. *Only in Canada You Say: A Treasury of Canadian Language*. Don Mills: Oxford University Press, 2007.

Casselman, Bill. *Canadian Sayings: A Comic Browse through Words and Folk Sayings Invented by Canadians*. Toronto: McArthur & Company, 1999.

—*Casselman's Canadian Words: 1,200 Folk Sayings Used by Canadians*. Toronto: McArthur & Company, 1999.

Farrow, Jane, ed. *Wanted Words: From Amalgamots to Undercarments—Language Gaps Found and Fixed*. Toronto: Stoddart Publishing, 2000.

—*Wanted Words 2: From Armajello to Yawncore: More Language Gaps Found and Fixed.* Toronto: Stoddart Publishing, 2001.

Gold, Elaine. "Canadian eh? A survey of contemporary use." Presented at the annual conference of the Canadian Linguistic Association, University of Manitoba, Winnipeg, 2004.

John, David, and Brian Kennedy. *How to Speak Hockey.* Arctic Raven, 2007.

Parkin, Tom. *Wet Coast Words.* Victoria: Orca Book Publishers, 1989.

Pratt, T.K., ed. *Dictionary of Prince Edward Island English.* Toronto: University of Toronto Press, 1996.

Pratt, T.K., and Scott Burke. *Prince Edward Island Sayings.* Toronto: University of Toronto Press, 1998.

Sandilands, John. *Western Canadian Dictionary and Phrase Book.* Edmonton: University of Alberta Press, 1977.

Story, G.M. with W.J. Kirwin and J.D.A. Widdowson, eds. *Dictionary of Newfoundland English: Second edition with supplement.* Toronto: University of Toronto Press, 1990.

Thay, Edrick. *Weird Canadian Words.* Edmonton: Folklore Press, 2004.

Web Sources

A note about Wikipedia: While everyone should be wary about information they encounter on the web, resources like Wikipedia can be useful and generally trusted when trying to ascertain well-documented, non-contentious facts of public record, such as the dates the *October Crisis* took place, or even the year that *Canadian Tire money* was first introduced. Although I have tried to use only print sources to research words and expressions, I turned to Wikipedia when I needed additional facts or context.

http://en.wikipedia.org/wiki/A_few_acres_of_snow

http://en.wikipedia.org/wiki/Canadian_English

http://en.wikipedia.org/wiki/Canadian_Legion

http://en.wikipedia.org/wiki/Canadian_raising

http://en.wikipedia.org/wiki/Canadian_Tire_money

http://en.wikipedia.org/wiki/Casey_and_Finnegan

http://en.wikipedia.org/wiki/Chasse-galerie

http://en.wikipedia.org/wiki/Chimo

http://en.wikipedia.org/wiki/Clamato

http://en.wikipedia.org/wiki/Coffee_crisp

http://en.wikipedia.org/wiki/Degrassi

http://en.wikipedia.org/wiki/Diefenbunker

http://en.wikipedia.org/wiki/Due_south

http://en.wikipedia.org/wiki/Eskimo_words_for_snow

http://en.wikipedia.org/wiki/Fuddle_duddle

http://en.wikipedia.org/wiki/Giants_of_the_Prairies

http://en.wikipedia.org/wiki/Heritage_Moments

http://en.wikipedia.org/wiki/Hockey_Night_in_Canada

http://en.wikipedia.org/wiki/Husky_Energy

http://en.wikipedia.org/wiki/I'se_the_B'y

http://en.wikipedia.org/wiki/Inco

http://en.wikipedia.org/wiki/Inuit_throat_singing

Notes on Sources

http://en.wikipedia.org/wiki/Joual

http://en.wikipedia.org/wiki/Katimavik

http://en.wikipedia.org/wiki/Kids_in_the_Hall

http://en.wikipedia.org/wiki/MAPL

http://en.wikipedia.org/wiki/Moving_Day

http://en.wikipedia.org/wiki/Nanook_of_the_North

http://en.wikipedia.org/wiki/National_Energy_Program

http://en.wikipedia.org/wiki/National_Film_Board_of_
Canada#Creation

http://en.wikipedia.org/wiki/Newfoundland_Screech

http://en.wikipedia.org/wiki/North_of_60

http://en.wikipedia.org/wiki/North_West_Company

http://en.wikipedia.org/wiki/O_Canada

http://en.wikipedia.org/wiki/October_Crisis

http://en.wikipedia.org/wiki/On-to-Ottawa_Trek

http://en.wikipedia.org/wiki/Red_Rose_Tea

http://en.wikipedia.org/wiki/Rhinoceros_Party

http://en.wikipedia.org/wiki/Sacre_bleu

http://en.wikipedia.org/wiki/Seigneurial_system_ of_New_
France

http://en.wikipedia.org/wiki/Smarties_(Nestl%C3%A9)

http://en.wikipedia.org/wiki/Stompin_Tom

http://en.wikipedia.org/wiki/Tim_Hortons

http://en.wikipedia.org/wiki/Tunit

http://en.wikipedia.org/wiki/Two_Solitudes

http://en.wikipedia.org/wiki/Wayne_and_Shuster

http://dooryard.ca/indexIntro.html

http://www.billcasselman.com/cwod_archive/eh.html

About the Author

Geordie Telfer

Geordie is a writer, actor, radio performer and artist in Toronto, Ontario. Geordie has been the assistant director for the Toronto Studio Players Theatre School, a freelance set carpenter, and a web and television writer. He worked extensively on deafplanet.com, the first TV show and website in American Sign Language, and has written several nature documentaries. Geordie has always been interested in words and how they are used. He has written two other nonfiction books, including *Real Canadian Pirates*.